# SPECTRUM

# Language Arts

## Grade 2

Dr. Betty Jane Wagner

McGraw-Hill
Consumer Products

## Author

**Betty Jane Wagner**

Professor
Reading and Language Department
National-Louis University
Evanston, IL

## Editorial Reviewer Board

Illustration
Steve McInturff

*McGraw-Hill*
*Consumer Products*

*A Division of The McGraw-Hill Companies*

Send all inquiries to:
McGraw-Hill Consumer Products
8787 Orion Place
Columbus, OH 43240-4027

Printed in the United States of America

ISBN 1-57768-472-9

1 2 3 4 5 6 7 8 9 10 GRAY 05 04 03 02 01 00

# Table of Contents

## Mechanics ................................................................................................................

# Usage ......................................................................

## Using the Appropriate Word

## Special Problems

# Grammar ...........................................................................

## Parts of Speech

## Sentences

## Writer's Handbook

## Answer Key

# 1 Capitalization: First Word in a Sentence

*Use a capital letter to begin each sentence. The capital is like a green traffic light. Go!*

### .................... Did You Know? ..........

**The capital letter at the beginning of each sentence often tells you that it is time to take a breath. Whew!**

Some snakes act like a baby's toy. They like to rattle.

## Show What You Know

**Circle each word below that should begin with a capital letter.**

a little snake could not see very well. he tried to wrap himself

around a tree. the tree began to walk. it was really an elephant's leg.

then the snake fell in love. his girlfriend turned out to be a garden hose.

now the snake wears glasses.

Score: _____     **Total Possible: 7**

# Proofread

**Read this story about an unlucky snake. Circle three letters that need to be capitalized. Write the capital letter above each one.**

**Example:** Ⓦe go to Ⓐunt Ann's house every Ⓣhanksgiving.

The little snake did not feel well. first, he bit his lip. then, he had a

frog in his throat. Finally, he took some aspirin. now he is much better.

# Practice

**Write two sentences about the picture. Do not forget to use capital letters.**

1. _____

   _____

2. _____

   _____

# Tips for Your Own Writing: Proofreading ..............

Look at a story you have written. Are you ready to **Go** at the beginning of each sentence? Did you begin each sentence with a capital letter?

*Begin each sentence in a big way—with a capital letter.*

# 2 Capitalization: The Word *I*

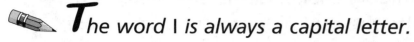

*T*he word I *is always a capital letter.*

## ·········· Did You Know? ·········

**You are a very important person. When you use *I* in place of your name, make it a capital letter.**

I love sports!
My dad and I play catch together.
So far the only thing I have caught is a cold!

# Show What You Know

**Read this poem. Circle each word *i* that should be a capital letter.**

My dad and i went fishing.

We went to Rainbow Lake.

i thought i'd catch a fish.

It would be a piece of cake.

i sat and sat for hours.

The fish just would not bite.

i finally told the worms,

"I'm going home. Good night."

**Score: _____      Total Possible: 5**

**8**

# Proofread

**Read each sentence below. Circle six letters that need to be capitals. Write the capital letter above each one.**

I am an insect, and i can do what I am. What am i? **i am a fly!**

i am round on the ends and high in the middle. What am i? **i am Ohio!**

# Practice

**Pretend that you are a football or soccer player. Write two sentences about what you would be doing. Do not forget to use capital letters!**

1. _____

_____

_____

2. _____

_____

_____

# Tips for Your Own Writing: Proofreading ..............

Read something you have written about yourself. Did you use a capital I when you talked about yourself?

 *Capital letters can be eye (I)—catching!*

# 3 Capitalization: People and Pets

*Your name makes you very special. People notice names because they begin with capital letters.*

## ........................ Did You Know? ..................

**A person's name or a pet's name always begins with a capital letter.**

> **M**ike and his dog **S**kimpy used an air pump at the gas station.
>
> **M**ike's dad told **M**ike to pump up **S**kimpy's air mattress.

# Show What You Know

**Circle each word below that should begin with a capital letter.**

The owners and their pets were ready to make the new movie.

allison walked her pet alligator choppers through the car wash to clean

his teeth. gordon and his pet gorilla harry climbed the jungle gym. libby

and her lion kitty took lots of catnaps. The movie starred my elephant

ellie and was a huge success!

Score: _____     Total Possible: 7

# Proofread

**Read the poem below. Circle seven letters that need to be capitalized. Then write the capital letter above each one.**

Sam has a snake named slinky.

It slides across the floor.

it goes for rex, a lizard,

but rex runs out the door.

jack owns a dog named Arf.

He loves a cat called Mew.

When arf and mew eat lunch,

they always chat and chew.

# Practice

**Write two sentences about people and their pets. Be sure to name each person and pet.**

1. _____

_____

_____

2. _____

_____

_____

# Tips for Your Own Writing: Proofreading ..............

Look at your own writing. Read something you have written about someone you know. Have you used a capital letter to begin every name?

 *Use capital letters for names.*

11

# 4 Capitalization: Titles of Relatives

*R*oyal families are not the only ones to have titles. People in **everyone's** family have titles. You are as special as a prince or a princess!

## ·············· Did You Know? ·····················

**A person's name always begins with a capital letter. When a title is added before a name, the title usually begins with a capital letter, too.**

> **U**ncle **F**arley **F**arkle and **A**unt **F**ranny **F**arkle fed peanuts to their cows. **U**ncle **F**arley and **A**unt **F**ranny hoped to get peanut butter instead of milk! The **F**arkles tend to be a little silly.

## Show What You Know

**Circle each word below that should begin with a capital letter.**

uncle Farley and aunt Franny invited their family to stay at the farm.

First, cousin Fifi Farkle and cousin Freddy Farkle came in their "pig-up"

truck. At midnight, grandpa Fletcher Farkle and grandma Frieda Farkle

finally arrived. grandpa Farkle had stopped to buy a hammer so that he

could hit the hay when he arrived.

Score: _____     Total Possible: 7

# Proofread

**Read the story below. Circle four words that need to begin with a capital letter. Then write the capital letter above each one.**

Everyone had fun on the Farkle farm. cousin Fifi helped Grandma

Farkle plant eggs to grow eggplants. cousin Freddy and grandpa Farkle

tried to play horseshoes with aunt Franny, but they could not get the

shoes off the horse.

# Practice

**Write two sentences about the Farkle relatives. Give each person a title and a name.**

1. _____

2. _____

# Tips for Your Own Writing: Proofreading ...............

Next time you write to someone in your family, check your titles. Did you remember that titles are capitalized when placed before names?

*Show your relatives that you think they are important. Use capital letters!*

# 5 Capitalization: Titles of Respect

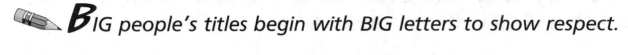 *BIG people's titles begin with BIG letters to show respect.*

### ·················· Did You Know? ··················

**Miss, Mrs., Ms., and Mr. are titles of respect and should be used before adult names. Begin each title with a capital letter.**

Mr. and Mrs. Rodeo
had a son named Buck.
He became a famous rider.
He was known as Mr. Buck.

## Show What You Know

**Circle each word below that should begin with a capital letter.**

mrs. Trotter rode her horse.

It bucked her in the air.

mr. Trotter caught his wife.

This gave her quite a scare!

mr. Trotter took his wife

And showed her how to ride.

He found a gentle horse for her.

Now mrs. Trotter rides with pride!

Score: _____       Total Possible: 4

# Proofread

**Read the poem below. Circle four letters that need to be capitalized. Write the capital letter above each one.**

Little miss Short likes to twirl

A rope around the cows.

Big mr. Stretch rides to win

And likes to take big bows.

mr. Steer and Mrs. Steer

Once tried to tame a bull.

mrs. Calf arrived to help,

But the bull had too much pull!

# Practice

**Write two sentences about these people: Miss Brand, Mrs. Chaps, Ms. Spurs, and Mr. Buckaroo.**

1. _____

_____

_____

2. _____

_____

_____

# Tips for Your Own Writing: Proofreading ..............

Next time you write a letter to an adult, be sure to show respect. Use capital letters for the title.

✎ *Show respect for adults in a **big** way! Use capital letters when you call them Miss, Mrs., Ms., or Mr.*

# 6 Review: Capitalization

**A. Read the paragraph below. Circle eleven letters that should be capitalized. Write the capital letter above each one.**

My little sister annie and i have a lot of fun together. we go to the

park almost every day in the summer. i like to swing. Annie likes to climb

on the monkey bars. When uncle lee and aunt Susie come to visit, they

go to the park with us. we usually pack a picnic lunch to take along.

they have as much fun as annie and i.

Score: _____    **Total Possible: 11**

**B. Read the sentences below. Circle ten letters that need to be capitalized. Write the capital letter above each one.**

**1.** mother goose took flying lessons from an eagle pilot.

**2.** little miss muffet went to the store to buy bug spray.

**3.** mr. and mrs. sprat loved to eat fast food.

**4.** mary and i took her lamb home from school.

Score: _____    **Total Possible: 10**

**C. Read the sentences below. Write the correct capital letter in each blank. You will use an *I*, *M*, or *G* for each blank.**

I just invented a magic pencil. _____y magic pencil did all my
                                      **1**

math homework for _____rs. Benson. _____ could not believe that all
                      **2**                        **3**

the math was correct! _____ wrote a letter to _____r. and
                          **4**                          **5**

_____rs. Lee in Chinese. _____ don't even know Chinese! When my
   **6**                          **7**

magic pencil broke its lead, it grew new lead. _____ wrote the
                                                   **8**

President a letter. The President invited me to visit him at the White

House. _____ showed my pencil to _____randpa Wise. _____randpa
          **9**                          **10**                      **11**

Wise told me that the magic really comes from my heart and my head.

Score: _____     Total Possible: 11

REVIEW SCORE: _____     REVIEW TOTAL: 32

# 7 Capitalization: Places

*Your writing will not go far if you do not place a capital letter at the beginning of names of places.*

......................... **Did You Know?** .....................

**There are many kinds of places. Use a capital letter for the first letter of the name of each special place.**

Sue visited the **K**alamazoo **Z**oo. (zoo)
Dinah is from **N**orth **C**arolina. (state)
Gail stayed overnight in **V**ail. (city)
Pete lives on **S**weet **S**treet. (street)
Jewel goes to **L**iverpool **S**chool. (school)
Erica was born in the **U**nited **S**tates of **A**merica. (country)

# Show What You Know

**Circle each word below that should begin with a capital.**

In america there really is a city called baker. It is in the state of

oregon. Do the children in baker attend chocolate cake school on

frosting street? We would have to visit oregon to find the answer.

Score: _____        **Total Possible: 10**

# Proofread

**Read this report about Disney World. Circle ten words that need to be capitalized. Write the capital letter above each one.**

Many people visit disney World in orlando, florida. A lot of these people come from the United states of america. You can visit disney world in other places in the world, too. Mickey Mouse and his friends are in tokyo, japan, and Paris, france.

# Practice

**Write a sentence that tells the city and state where you live. Write another sentence that tells the name of your school.**

1. _____

_____

2. _____

# Tips for Your Own Writing: Proofreading ..............

Next time you write about a special place, be sure to use a capital letter to begin the names of countries, states, cities, and streets.

 *Begin each trip to a special place with a capital letter.*

# 8 Capitalization: Days and Months

*Mark your calendar with capitals! Begin days of the week and months of the year with capital letters.*

## Did You Know?

**There are seven days in the week and twelve months in a year. Those nineteen words always begin with a capital letter.**

**S**unday, **M**onday, **T**uesday, **W**ednesday, **T**hursday, **F**riday, **S**aturday

**J**anuary, **F**ebruary, **M**arch, **A**pril, **M**ay, **J**une, **J**uly, **A**ugust, **S**eptember, **O**ctober, **N**ovember, **D**ecember

## Show What You Know

**Read this poem. Circle each letter that should be capitalized.**

On monday Millie made a cake.

She slept all day and it did bake.

On Tuesday Tony saw the smoke

And shook his sister till she woke.

That was april of last year

Or so I heard from sister dear.

If Millie made a pie in june

Will it not be ready soon?

Score: _____     Total Possible: 3

# Proofread

**Read each riddle below. Circle each letter that needs to be capitalized. Write the capital letter above it. There are three mistakes.**

**1.** Why is sunday the smartest day of the week? **It is the brightest.**

**2.** Why do soldiers dislike march? **It hurts their feet.**

**3.** When is may a polite month? **When it is used with the words "I**

**please."**

# Practice

**Write one sentence about the day of the week you like best. Write another sentence to tell which month you like best.**

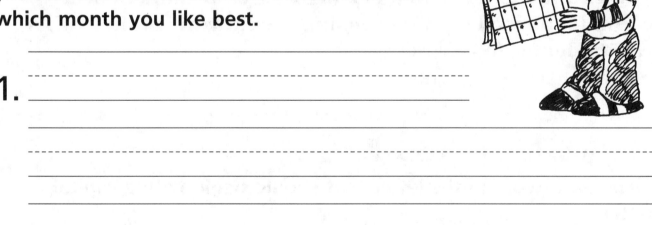

**1.** _____

_____

_____

**2.** _____

# Tips for Your Own Writing: Proofreading . . . . . . . . . . . . . .

Reread a journal entry. Did you begin your day of the week and month of the year with capital letters?

*S*tart each day of the week and each month of the year with a smile . . . and a capital letter!

# 9 Capitalization: Friendly Letters

*Friendly letters are letters you write to friends. Use capital letters for important parts of friendly letters.*

## ........................... Did You Know? ....................

**Friendly letters begin with the date at the top. Always use a capital letter for the name of the month—A**ugust 10, 2000.

**Start your greeting with *Dear*. Then write your friend's name. Begin each word with a capital—D**ear **P**atrick,

**The body of the letter is what you want to tell your friend. Use capital letters to begin each sentence.**

**You end the letter with a closing and your name. Use a capital letter to begin the closing. Begin your name with a capital letter, too—S**incerely,
                    **C**indy

## Show What You Know

**Circle each word in the letter that should begin with a capital letter.**

february 20, 2000

dear brad,

    my mother took me to the eye doctor yesterday. the doctor said I needed glasses.

                    your friend,
                    john

Score: _____     **Total Possible: 7**

# Proofread

**Read the letter below. Circle seven letters that should be capitalized. Write the capital letter above each one.**

november 10, 2000

dear jimmy,

i work like a horse. i eat like a bird. i am as tired as a

dog. Everyone tells me to see a vet.

Sincerely,

Sam smith

# Practice

**Think of a relative. Write a greeting and the first sentence of a friendly letter to that relative.**

1. _____

2. _____

# Tips for Your Own Writing: Proofreading ..............

The next time you write a letter, look at the important parts. Did you use capitals for them?

*Make your letters "letter-perfect." Capitals show what is important!*

# 10 Review: Capitalization

**A. Read Samantha's letter below. Circle 21 letters that should be capitalized. Write the capital letter above each one.**

july 29, 2000

dear Mom and Dad,

    today is tuesday. camp Swampy is really neat. All the

bugs are very big. i have a spider named fuzzy. her legs

have a lot of hair. i put her in a jar on monday. spike is my

snake. he sleeps with me in my sleeping bag. kyle, the

adult who stays in my tent, doesn't know about spike. i

will show you spike and fuzzy when I come home in

august. i cannot wait to see what I will find tomorrow!

    love,

    samantha

**Score: _____ Total Possible: 21**

**B. Read Joshua's letter below. Circle each letter that should be capitalized. Write the capital letter above each one. There are 22 letters to capitalize.**

june 16, 2000

dear Grandma and Grandpa,

    i miss you so much! do you think spot will remember me? i know that you will think I have grown taller. i hope that tommy, my friend on oak avenue, will still be my friend. i hope my bike is not rusty. i started this letter two days ago. mom says that I should mail it today. on friday we are going to mount rushmore in south dakota. we will meet some really big presidents. See you later!

love,

joshua

Score: _____      Total Possible: 22

REVIEW SCORE: _____      REVIEW TOTAL: 43

# 11 Punctuation: Periods

*Use a period to end a sentence that tells something. It is like a stop sign.* **Stop.**

## ·················· Did You Know? ··················

**A period at the end of a sentence shows you that a statement is finished.**

Cows like to dance so that they can make milk shakes.

Chickens like to spin around so that they can make scrambled eggs.

## Show What You Know

**Put a slash (/) at the end of each sentence.**

Animals and people might have funny favorite foods  An elephant

may like squash  Some fish may choose watermelon  Sheep may be very

happy to get baa-nanas  Goats eat canned anything  Scared people may

eat chicken  My favorite food is hay because I eat like a horse

Score: _____    Total Possible: 7

# Proofread

**Read the story below. Five periods are missing. Circle the words that should have periods after them.**

Oscar was very hungry He decided to make a big sandwich. First, he got a huge loaf of bread Then, he added some ham and cheese. Next, he put on some pickles Oscar added bananas, strawberries, and whipped cream. Oscar took a bite His sandwich did not taste very good

# Practice

**Write two sentences that tell something about a game you like. End each sentence with a period.**

1. _____

2. _____

# Tips for Your Own Writing: Proofreading ..............

Look at something you have written. Did you use a period to end each telling sentence?

*Don't forget to **stop** at the end of a telling sentence with a period.*

# 12 Punctuation: Question Marks

*Use a question mark to end a sentence that asks something.*

## ........................ Did You Know?.....

**Sentences that ask questions end with a question mark.**

> Why did the cow jump over the moon**?**
> He wanted to get to the Milky Way.

## Show What You Know

**Read the story below. There should be a question mark after each asking sentence. Circle each word that should have a question mark after it.**

Starry Knight was an astronaut. She was ready to fly into space.

Where did she put her food It was in her launch box. Did she forget

anything Starry brought a mop to clean up any stardust. What was

missing Starry ran to get a shovel. She might need to dig a black hole.

Would the trip be interesting Ms. Knight would soon find out.

Score: _____     Total Possible: 4

# Proofread

**Read the story below. Circle three words that should have question marks after them.**

Starry Knight's rocket blasted off. She landed on a new planet.

Would she meet strange creatures Would they be friendly Starry climbed

out of the rocket. She saw a purple, three-headed creature. What was it?

Was it friendly It told her that it liked to eat vegetables. It asked if she

were a vegetable. Starry Knight left quickly.

# Practice

**Write two asking sentences about outer space. Put a question mark at the end of each sentence.**

1. _____

_____

2. _____

# Tips for Your Own Writing: Proofreading .............

Check some of your writing to find asking sentences. Did you end each one with a question mark?

*Question marks ask questions like teachers do. Who knows the answers?*

# 13 Punctuation: Periods and Question Marks

✏️ *S*top at the end of each sentence. If the sentence tells something, use a period. If the sentence asks something, use a question mark.

.......................... **Did You Know?** .......

**Telling sentences always end with a period. Asking sentences always end with a question mark.**

Why is the dinosaur stopping**?**
He came to the end of the road**.**

. . . . . . . . . . . . . . . . . . . . . . . . . . . . . . . . . . . . . . . . . . .

## Show What You Know

**Underline each telling sentence. Circle each asking sentence.**

Mother Dinosaur was cleaning house She wanted Father Dinosaur

to help move some of the large rocks around the cave How would he do

this What would be the easiest way to help Mother Dinosaur Father

Dinosaur thought and thought What should he do Finally, he decided to

eat lots of spinach Then he could use his own dino-mite

Score: _____     **Total Possible: 8**

# Proofread

**Most riddles begin with an asking sentence and end with a telling sentence. Read each dinosaur riddle. Write a 1 before the asking part of the riddle and add a question mark at the end where it is needed. Write a 2 before the telling part of the riddle and add a period at the end where it is needed.**

_____ 1 _____ What is a stegosaurus's favorite sport

_____ 2 _____ Volleyball, because she can spike the ball

_____ 3 _____ She stood too close to the pencil sharpener

_____ 4 _____ How did the triceratops get pointy horns

# Practice

**Write one question and one statement about dinosaurs.**

1. _____

2. _____

# Tips for Your Own Writing: Proofreading ..............

Read a piece of your writing. Did you put a period after each telling sentence and a question mark after each asking sentence?

_Sentences, like stories, need correct endings. Otherwise they do not make sense._

# 14 Punctuation: Exclamation Points

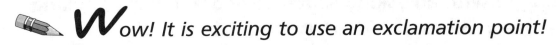 *Wow! It is exciting to use an exclamation point!*

## Did You Know?

**Sentences that show surprise or excitement end with an exclamation point. Read exclamatory sentences louder than others and use lots of expression!**

Look out**!** Something with four eyes and sixteen legs is climbing up the house**!**

## Show What You Know

**Read each set of sentences. Circle each sentence that shows excitement and should end with an exclamation point.**

King Kong just stepped on our piano and the keys went flat.

We play the piano at home.

Mom is washing our clothes.

Something is moving in the laundry basket.

A foot has twelve inches.

Big Foot is hiding behind that tree.

Score: _____     **Total Possible: 3**

# Proofread

**Read the poem below. Add one period and two exclamation points where they are needed.**

My friend and I went swimming.

We swam a long, long while.

We floated and we splashed about.

And then we saw a crocodile

The croc swam 'round in circles.

We were sad to leave so soon

It was 11:55.

And crocodiles eat at noon

# Practice

**Write two exciting sentences about something you have done. Be sure to end each sentence with an exclamation point.**

1. _____

2. _____

# Tips for Your Own Writing: Proofreading ..............

Read aloud with expression a story you have written. Did you use exclamation points for your exciting sentences?

*Exclamation points are like periods that explode with excitement!*

# 15 Review: Punctuation

**A. Read the poem below about cats. Add seven missing periods, three question marks, and two exclamation points.**

Tom the tomcat moved to town

He was acting tough

What did others think of Tom

He was mean and rough

Wise the dog soon heard of Tom

He could make things right

The dog would talk to Tom

Would Tom really want to fight

Tom listened to the dog

Wise was really smart

Did Tom learn he should be kind

Yes, he had a change of heart

Score: _____    Total Possible: 12

**B. Read the sentences below about clowns. Add four missing periods, two question marks, and two exclamation points.**

Willy, Billy, and Lily are circus clowns

Who is the silliest clown

Willy has a squirting flower

Oh no, he squirted me in the eye

Billy has big, big shoes

Billy just stepped on my foot

When Lily sings, her ears wiggle

Who is the silliest clown

Score: _____     Total Possible: 8

**C. Read the following sentences. Mixed-up Martha ended four sentences with the wrong marks. Circle each wrong mark and write the correct one at the end.**

Greta Green grew grapes!

Her friend Fried F. Frost fished?

Both bought books about boats.

Why.

Wanda and Wendy wondered?

Super Sally said she knew.

Do you?

Score: _____     Total Possible: 8

REVIEW SCORE: _____     REVIEW TOTAL: 28

# 16 Punctuation: Dates, Cities, States

✎ **C**ommas are sometimes used between words in sentences. *They tell the reader to pause for a very short time before finishing the sentence.*

### ........................ Did You Know? .....................

**A comma goes between the day and the year.**

How old will you be on January 1, 2100

**A comma goes between the name of a city and state. A comma also goes after the state if it is in the middle of a sentence.**

A train just left the station in Boston, Massachusetts, with the President on board.

## Show What You Know

**Read this paragraph. Put a slash (/) between each day and year. Also put a slash between the names of cities and states.**

The train arrived in Albany  New York, on March 13  2000. It

continued down the track until it reached Philadelphia  Pennsylvania. It

was sidetracked there until March 15  2000. The train finally arrived in

Baltimore  Maryland, on March 19  2000. From there, the train brought

the President home to the White House.

Score: _____          Total Possible: 6

# Proofread

**Add five commas where they are needed.**

My class was studying about unusual names of cities in the United States. I began my report on February 6 2000. I read about Boulder Colorado. I wonder if the rocks in that city are bigger than the rocks in Little Rock, Arkansas. Do ghosts really live in Casper Wyoming? Does everyone sew in Needles California? I finished my report on February 12, 2000. By the way, I live in Reading Pennsylvania.

# Practice

**Write a sentence that tells your birth date. Then write another sentence that names your city and state.**

1. _____

_____

2. _____

# Tips for Your Own Writing: Proofreading ..............

Look at a report you have written. Did you put a comma between the day and year, and also between the city and state?

*Commas make reading easier to understand. Pause when you see a comma!*

# 17 Punctuation: Commas in Friendly Letters

 *Commas are used in friendly letters. They tell the reader to pause.*

## ......................... Did You Know? .......................

**Put a comma between the day and year in the date—**January 4, 2000

**Put a comma after a greeting.**
Dear Cinderella,

**Put a comma after a closing.**
Love,
Prince Charming

## Show What You Know

**Read this letter. Put a slash (/) where commas are needed.**

> September 17  1598
>
> Dear Rapunzel
>
>     I have heard that you have the longest hair in the
>
> kingdom. Why do you let the prince climb up your hair?
>
> Shouldn't he get the elevator fixed?
>
>             Your friend
>
>             Sleeping Beauty

Score: _____     Total Possible: 3

# Proofread

**Add two commas where they are needed.**

September 25 1598

Dear Sleeping Beauty,

   The prince climbed my hair only once. He had to go chase a dragon. He had stopped at the market first to buy a fire alarm. (We finally got the elevator fixed!)

Sincerely

Rapunzel

# Practice

**Write a date, a greeting, and a closing for a letter. Don't forget the commas!**

Date: _____

Greeting: _____

Closing: _____

Writer's Name: _____

# Tips for Your Own Writing: Proofreading .............

Next time you write a friendly letter, read it aloud. Did you pause a little after the commas in the date, the greeting, and the closing?

✏ *Commas in letter parts show readers where to slow down and take a quick breath. Commas are for pausing.*

# 18 Punctuation: Commas in Lists

*Commas are used in lists of three or more. They let you know there are more than two items that belong together.*

## ..................... Did You Know? .........

**A comma goes between each person, place, thing, or phrase in a list.**

Did you hear about the Big Mac-Intosh computer? It comes with a bun, burger, cheese, lettuce, and special sauce!

## Show What You Know

**The story below is confusing. Help the story make sense by putting a slash (/) to show where commas are needed between the words or phrases in the lists.**

Dad sent me to the store to buy a melon  a cucumber  some olives

and some sugar. When I got to the store, I could not remember what I

was supposed to get. I knew something was round  something was long

something could fit on my fingers  and something was sweet. So I bought

a ball  a bat  a ring  and some candy.

Score: _____     Total Possible: 9

# Proofread

**Read each sentence below. Make the lists in the sentences easier to read by putting seven commas where they are needed.**

**1.** Fleas flies bees and beetles drive Bertha buggy.

**2.** What is slimy, slippery sloppy sluggish, and silver? I do not know, but

it is sitting on top of your head!

**3.** Mrs. Bryant sometimes confuses the names of her quadruplets Bruce

Brice, Brian and Bruno.

# Practice

**Make a list of three favorite foods and three favorite toys. Write one sentence that lists your favorite foods. Write another sentence that lists your favorite toys.**

**1.** _____

_____

_____

_____

**2.** _____

# Tips for Your Own Writing: Proofreading ..............

Find a list of things that you have written. Read the list aloud. Did you remember to add commas to separate the items in your list?

 ***A** comma is a pause that clears up confusion in a list.*

# 19 Punctuation: Commas in Compound Sentences

✎ *A comma used with **and, but**, or **or** can combine two sentences into one.*

......................... **Did You Know?** ..........

**Commas can link two complete sentences together if the words** *and*, *but*, **or** *or* **are used between the sentences.**

> Cats do not like to swim.
> Elephants always bring their trunks.
> Cats do not like to swim, **but** elephants
>    always bring their trunks.

............................................

# Show What You Know

**Read each sentence below. Circle the** *and*, *but*, **or** *or* **only if it connects two complete sentences. Then put a slash (/) where a comma should be added.**

**1.** Leopards have spots  but zebras have stripes.

**2.** Tigers are wild cats  and lions are wild cats.

**3.** Zebras and horses have similar bodies.

**4.** Do parrots understand what they say  or do parrots just copy the

   sounds of words?

**Score:** _____    **Total Possible: 6**

# Proofread

**Read the story below about people and animals. Four commas are needed where *and*, *but*, or *or* connects two sentences.**

My mother tells me people are a lot like animals but they try to be different. Humans do not like to look wrinkled but elephants are wrinkled all over. People wear black suits, and penguins look like they wear black suits. People carry hairbrushes but porcupines wear their hairbrushes. Do animals copy people or do people copy animals?

# Practice

**Think about two things you like to do. Put them together in one sentence. Use a comma and a connecting word.**

_____

-----------------------------------------

_____

-----------------------------------------

_____

-----------------------------------------

_____

# Tips for Your Own Writing: Proofreading ..............

Next time you want to combine two sentences, be sure to use **and, but, or or.** Place a comma in front of the connecting word.

 *Compound sentences can be twice as nice!*

# 20 Review: Commas

**A. Read about Goldilocks below. Add seven commas where they are needed.**

Goldilocks was lost in the forest. She came to a house and went in. She thought that the bowls of porridge were too hot too cold and just right. The three chairs felt too hard too soft and just right. The beds felt the same way and Goldilocks fell asleep. The Bear family came home and Goldilocks ran away. Then Goldilocks visited her grandma and her grandma told her to write a letter to the Bears.

Score: _____     Total Possible: 7

**B. Add nine commas where they are needed in Goldilocks's letter.**

June 10 2000

Dear Bear Family

I got lost in the forest and I went in your house because I was scared. I am sorry that I ate your porridge sat in your chairs and slept in your beds. Will you visit me in Honeyville Maine? We have lots of fruit nuts and honey.

Sincerely

Goldilocks

Score: _____     Total Possible: 9

**C. Read the rhyming sentences below. Then add thirteen commas.**

Papa Bear Mama Bear and Baby Bear all rode on a plane. They slept

most of the ride but they awoke in Honeyville Maine.

Goldilocks met them at the airport and she grinned from ear to ear.

They shook hands with her smiled at her and shouted a loud cheer.

At home they ate apples oranges berries nuts and pears. A new

friendship began for a girl and the three bears.

They will remember August 10 2000. They had a nice party and

Goldilocks turned seven!

Score: _____          **Total Possible: 13**

**REVIEW SCORE:** _____          **REVIEW TOTAL: 29**

# 21 Punctuation: Quotation Marks in Dialogue

*Use quotation marks around words that someone says aloud. It is like the words are surrounded!*

......................... **Did You Know?** .......

**Quotation marks go before and after a speaker's words.**

> The reptile roared, "I am the great Lizard of Oz!"
> The reptile's mother said, "You still need to eat your carrots, dear."

## Show What You Know

**Read the sentences below. Circle each speaker's exact words.**

**1.** Does anybody have some glue? asked Humpty Dumpty.

**2.** We are so hungry that we could eat a house! said Hansel and Gretel.

**3.** Cinderella asked Prince Charming, Are you a shoe salesman?

**4.** Don't wolf down your food! exclaimed Little Red Riding Hood.

**5.** The White Rabbit said, Digital watches are best.

Score: _____     Total Possible: 5

# Proofread

**Read the story below. Four sentences are missing quotation marks around the speaker's exact words. Circle those words.**

I am going to the market, said Mother Pig.

One little piggy fussed, I want to stay home!

Another little piggy asked, "Will you please buy me a cookie?"

The next little piggy cried, I never get anything!

Mom, I will be playing baseball! yelled the last little piggy.

# Practice

**Complete the sentences below by writing what might have been said. Put quotation marks around the words you wrote.**

1. The dragon said, _____

_____

_____

_____

2. _____ *yelled the giant.*

# Tips for Your Own Writing: Proofreading ..............

Next time you write a story and your characters say something, use quotation marks around the exact words each speaker says.

*I said, "Use quotation marks. Make people notice what is said!"*

# 22 Punctuation: Colons in Time

*It is time to tell time! A colon comes in "handy" when telling time!*

........................ **Did You Know?** ....................

**Use a colon between the hour and the minutes.**
**This makes it easier to read and understand.**

> The garbage collector gets sad every day at
>    3:15 p.m. That is when he is down in the
>    dumps.
> The zookeeper was hopping mad at 6:35 p.m.
>    His prize frog was flying a lily pad.

## Show What You Know

**Read these sentences that talk about jobs and time. Put a slash (/) between the hour and the minutes of each time to show where a colon is missing.**

**1.** The baker quit his job at 805 a.m. because he could not make enough

dough.

**2.** The lawyer dressed for court at 900 a.m. He wore his best lawsuit.

**3.** At 430 p.m. the mattress salesman was caught lying down on the job.

**4.** The mechanic fixed the radio at 1130 a.m. He gave it a tune-up.

Score: _____     **Total Possible: 4**

# Proofread

**Read the poem below. Put in three slashes to show where colons are missing.**

Uncle Goof fixed our roof with a special glue.

A storm began! The glue all ran at 2 22 a.m.!

Grandfather Moore fixed our door at 10 28 p.m.

We've lost our grin. We're still locked in. We must just sit and wait!

Auntie Jinx fixes sinks. She thinks she can repair.

At 6 00 p.m. we all see water squirting in the air!

# Practice

**Write two sentences that have a time in them. Include *a.m.* for a time from midnight to before noon. Include *p.m.* for a time from noon to before midnight.**

1. _____

2. _____

# Tips for Your Own Writing: Proofreading .............

Next time you go somewhere, write a note to leave behind. Tell what time you will be back. Remember to put a colon between the hour and the minutes.

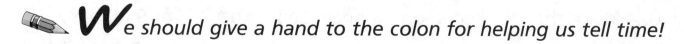 *We should give a hand to the colon for helping us tell time!*

# 23 Punctuation: Periods in Abbreviations

*Some words can be shortened. They end with a period. These words are called* abbreviations.

## ...................... Did You Know? .....................

**Some words can be shortened or abbreviated.**

**Days of the week and months of the year can be abbreviated only when used in a date. May, June, and July have no abbreviation.**

| | | |
|---|---|---|
| Sunday—**Sun.** | Tuesday—**Tues.** | Thursday—**Thurs.** |
| Monday—**Mon.** | Wednesday—**Wed.** | Friday—**Fri.** |
| | | Saturday—**Sat.** |

| | | |
|---|---|---|
| January—**Jan.** | April—**Apr.** | October—**Oct.** |
| February—**Feb.** | August—**Aug.** | November—**Nov.** |
| March—**Mar.** | September—**Sept.** | December—**Dec.** |

**People's titles can be abbreviated only when used with a name.**

| | | |
|---|---|---|
| Mister—**Mr.** | Mistress—**Mrs.** | Doctor—**Dr.** |

**Types of streets can be abbreviated only when used as part of the name of a street.**

| | | |
|---|---|---|
| Street—**St.** | Avenue—**Ave.** | Drive—**Dr.** |

**Types of measurement can be abbreviated only when used after a number. Most do not need a period.**

| | | |
|---|---|---|
| pound(s)—**lb(s)** | inch(es)—**in.** | minute(s)—**min** |

## Show What You Know

**Circle each word that can be abbreviated.**

Mister Tommy Turtle was getting ready for the big race on Runway Road. He lifted weights that were 2 pounds each. He drank 3 ounces of juice. Finally, the race began on Monday, September 15, at 9:00 a.m.

**Score:** _____ **Total Possible: 6**

# Proofread

**Read the story below. Circle the five abbreviations that are missing periods.**

Mr Jack Rabbit lived alone at 83 Hutch Ave. His life was good, but he was lonely. Everything changed on Feb 13, 2000. Miss Bunny Hare was visiting friends on a nearby street. Jack saw Bunny, and they fell in love. They were married on Fri, Feb. 14, by Rev Cottontail. Bunny carried 3 lbs of carrots for a bouquet. The next day Mr. Jack Rabbit and Mrs Bunny Rabbit went on a bunnymoon.

# Practice

**Write a sentence in which you use an abbreviation in your street address. Write another sentence in which you use an abbreviation in your birth date.**

1. _____

_____

2. _____

# Tips for Your Own Writing: Proofreading ..............

Next time you write a letter to an adult, look at the title of respect. Did you abbreviate it and use a period?

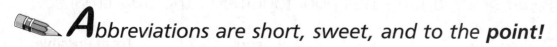

*bbreviations are short, sweet, and to the point!*

# 24 Punctuation: Apostrophes in Possessives

*When you want to show others that something belongs to you, use an apostrophe.*

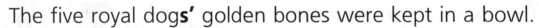

.................... Did You Know? ....................

**An apostrophe is used to show that someone owns something.**

**When there is one owner, use 's.**

The prince**'s** golden baseball is kept in a fancy case.

**When there is more than one owner, usually use s'.**

The five royal dog**s'** golden bones were kept in a bowl.

. . . . . . . . . . . . . . . . . . . . . . . . . . . . . . . . . . . . . . . .

## Show What You Know

**Read the story below. Circle each word that needs an apostrophe to show ownership.**

Lonely, Princess Penny was playing by the kings pond. A frog

jumped up on a lily pad and croaked, "It is the kings pond, but these are

all the frogs rocks. You may walk on them and play with us."

Princess Penny kissed the frogs head, and she turned into a frog!

"Now we can swim in the kings pool together!" the frog croaked.

Score: _____     Total Possible: 5

# Proofread

**Read the poem below. Circle three words that are missing apostrophes to show ownership.**

The kings gold was in the treasury.

The queen's jewels were in a box.

The royal baby lay asleep.

He had the chicken pox.

The doctors bottles of medicine

Were kept so nice and cold.

The medicine was special.

The princes pox were made of gold.

# Practice

**Write two sentences that show ownership. Do not forget to use 's or s' in each sentence.**

1. _____

_____

_____

2. _____

# Tips for Your Own Writing: Proofreading ...............

Next time you write about something that is owned, remember to use an apostrophe. Use 's for one owner and s' for more than one owner.

**A**n apostrophe is proof of ownership. Be sure to use it wisely!

# 25 Punctuation: Underlining Titles

*Underline the titles of books and movies when you are writing their names.*

### ····················· Did You Know? ·····················

**The titles of books and movies are underlined or put in italics. Underlining helps you find them in the sentence.**

After I saw the movie The Little Mermaid, I decided to call my friends and go swimming.

## Show What You Know

**Read the story below. Underline each title.**

The animals were discussing their favorite books and movies. Brandi Bunny loved reading Carrot Seed. Freddie Fox mentioned Chicken Soup with Rice. Then Kitty Cat talked about reading Mouse Soup, but she decided to be quiet when Mortimer Mouse wrinkled his nose. Woody Wolf licked his lips and raved about seeing The Three Little Pigs ten times. He also said that he never stays for the ending. Everyone suddenly was hungry for lunch.

Score: _____     Total Possible: 4

# Proofread

**Read each sentence below. Add the missing lines under four book and movie titles.**

**1.** After I saw Aladdin, I wished I had a genie for my friend.

**2.** My dad should read Arthur's Eyes before he gets his new glasses.

**3.** We went to see <u>The Lion King</u> ten times.

**4.** Sharon gave her brother Butch the book Beauty and the Beast for his birthday. He did not laugh.

**5.** Our mail carrier thinks The Jolly Postman is a great book.

# Practice

**Write two sentences about your favorite books and movies. Do not forget to underline the titles.**

**1.** _____

_____

**2.** _____

# Tips for Your Own Writing: Proofreading ..............

Look at a book report you have written. Are the titles underlined?

_L_anguage Roundup *can help you become a better writer.*

# 26 Review: Punctuation

**A. Read the story below. Circle the set of words in five sentences where quotation marks should be used, put three slashes (/) where colons are missing in time, and put a box around three places where periods are missing in abbreviations.**

Mrs Fritzi Frazzle sat working at her computer.

It was already 345 p.m., and she had not finished her work.

I will never be done by 600 p.m., she said to herself.

Suddenly a spider crawled across her screen.

Eeeek! screamed Fritzi.

Shhh! said the spider. I am looking for flies to go with my burger.

Fritzi left the room. She returned with bug repellent. She sprayed near the computer.

Fritzi happily said, Mrs Fritzi Frazzle's computer has no bugs in it!

She went back to work. She finished at 558 p.m. on Mon, August 16.

**Score:** _____     **Total Possible: 11**

B. **Read the story. Circle the set of words in seven sentences where quotation marks should be used, put two slashes (/) where colons are missing in time, box five words where apostrophes are needed to show ownership, and add one underline under a title.**

Mom, what time is it? asked Buffy.

Her mom answered, It is 202. That's two minutes later than the last time you asked.

Will we get to the movie on time? Buffy asked.

Sure, we will. We will meet Mrs. McMann and Muffy at the theater. Muffys brother Murphy may come, too, answered Buffys mom.

Yuk! Murphys manners are disgusting! exclaimed Buffy. She yawned loudly.

They arrived at the movie at 215 p.m. Buffy was asleep. Buffys mom woke her, and Buffy dragged herself into the theater.

Everyone sat down. Buffy slept all the way through Sleeping Beauty. She snored.

Mom, said Murphy, Buffys manners are disgusting!

Score: _____     **Total Possible: 15**

**REVIEW SCORE: _____**     **REVIEW TOTAL: 26**

# 27 Usage: Verbs–Has, Have

✏️ *In this lesson, you'll find out when to use* has *and when to use* have.

## ···················· Did You Know? ·····················

A verb is a word that tells what the subject of the sentence does.

Use *has* when you are talking about one subject.

> Jo **has** a shadow.

Use *have* when you are talking about yourself or more than one subject.

> I **have** a shadow, too.
> My friends **have** two shadows.

## Show What You Know

**Read the sentences below. Fill in each blank with *has* or *have.***

I _____ a shy shadow. I think it _____ a hiding place.
       1                                2

It also _____ many shapes. I _____ only one. My shadow
        3                       4

and I _____ a good time together.
    5

Score: _____      Total Possible: 5

# Proofread

**This letter has five mistakes. Draw a line through each incorrect word. Write the correct word above it.**

**Example:** The birds ~~has~~ <sup>have</sup> colorful feathers.

Dear Uncle Jack,

    I has  a new bird. It have beautiful feathers. Its tail have red

feathers, and its wings has  blue and green feathers. The bird have a

name. It's Loud Mouth!

                Love,

                Joey

# Practice

**Write one sentence about something you have. Write one sentence about something a friend has.**

1. _____

2. _____

# Tips for Your Own Writing: Proofreading................

The next time you write a letter, look for the verbs *has* and *have*. Have you used them correctly?

 **Y**ou (*has*, <u>*have*</u>) *studied about* has *and* have.

# 28 Usage: Verbs—Is, Are

✏️ *Get ready to learn something new about two words you use every day.*

................. **Did You Know?** ....................

**Is** and *are* are verbs. They tell what the subject is.

**Use *is* when you are talking about one subject.**

Kim **is** the class clown.

**Use *are* when you are talking about more than one subject.**

Ben and Lia **are** funny, too.

•••••••••••••••••••••••••••••••••••••••

# Show What You Know

**Read the sentences below. Fill in each blank with *is* or *are*.**

Ben and Lia _____ silly. So _____ Kim. He _____
                    1                          2                    3

really an actor. They _____ all in the class play. It _____
                              4                                           5

about animals that learn to talk.

Score: _____        Total Possible: 5

# Proofread

**This story has four mistakes. Draw a line through each incorrect word. Write the correct word above it.**

**Example:** The children ~~is~~ <sup>are</sup> in the park.

Ben and Lia is very friendly. They is happiest when they are with

their friends. Kim does not like to be alone. He is under a big oak tree

waiting for Ben and Lia. He are lonely. Here come Ben and Lia. They is

on their way.

# Practice

**Write one sentence about your friend. Write another one about the two of you. Use *is* in one sentence and *are* in the other one.**

1.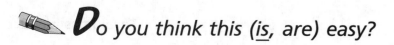

2. 

# Tips for Your Own Writing: Proofreading ..............

Look for the verbs *is* and *are* in a story you have written. Have you used *is* with one subject and *are* with more than one?

*D*o you think this (*is*, are) easy?

# 29 Usage: Verbs—Was, Were

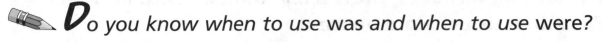 *Do you know when to use* was *and when to use* were?

......................... **Did You Know?** ....................

*Was* and *were* are verbs. They tell what something or someone is or is like.

Use *was* when you are talking about yourself or one subject.

> Jeff **was** a comedian.
> I **was** his partner.

Use *were* when you are talking about more than one subject.

> Ash and Kawa **were** the funniest.

## Show What You Know

**Read the poem below. If an underlined word is incorrect, cross it out and write the correct word above it.**

We <u>was</u> on the beach.
   1

I ran with my friend Lin.

We <u>were</u> like the wind.
   2

Lin stopped to get a shell,

A shell so long and thin.

It <u>were</u> just out of reach.
   3

Then the water came.

The shell <u>was</u> out to sea again.
   4

Score: _____     **Total Possible: 2**

# Proofread

**This story has three mistakes. Draw a line through each incorrect word. Write the correct word above it.**

**Example:** We ~~was~~ <sup>were</sup> on time.

Jared was in the lunchroom. His lunch were at home on the kitchen

counter. His parents was at work. Jared were hungry.

# Practice

**Write two sentences telling about what happened when you have forgotten something. Use *was* or *were* in each sentence.**

1. _____

_____

_____

2. _____

_____

_____

# Tips for Your Own Writing: Proofreading ..............

Read a piece of your writing. Look for the verbs *was* and *were*. Did you use *was* with one subject and *were* with more than one?

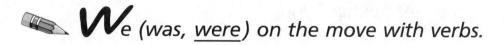 *We (was, _were_) on the move with verbs.*

# 30 Review: Verbs

## A. Circle the verbs *is* and *are.*

This is a funny bus

With zebra stripes and polka dots,

A driver who is Gus,

And a hundred plants in pots.

Gus is on a fuzzy seat,                    The bus is on its way to school,

And numbers one through ten          Gus seems as happy as can be.

Are with her best friend Pete.          She is able to keep her cool.

Behind are letters that look like men.   There is so much to see.

**Score:** _____  **Total Possible: 8**

## B. Write *is* or *are* in each blank.

1. A fish _____ on another seat.

2. Shapes _____ in the aisle.

3. Imagine you _____ on the bus.

4. What _____ on the seat behind you?

**Score:** _____  **Total Possible: 4**

**C. Write *was* or *were* in each blank.**

The leaves _____ all over the yard. Tom raked them into a
                  **1**

big pile. His little brother _____ there. He _____ happy.
                             **2**                **3**

When Tom finished, they ran toward the pile. The pile _____ deep.
                                                       **4**

Then they disappeared. Out they popped! Tom and his brother

_____ happy.
**5**

Score: _____          Total Possible: 5

**D. Read this paragraph. Look for *has* and *have.* If the word is used incorrectly, draw a line through it. Write the correct word above it. There are four mistakes.**

Della and Steve has a plan. They head for the kitchen. Della have

the milk. Steve have the ice cream. Della has the glasses and the spoons.

Della and Steve has  chocolate syrup. What are they making?

Score: _____          Total Possible: 4

REVIEW SCORE: _____          REVIEW TOTAL: 21

# 31 Usage: Verbs–Ran, Run

*B*oth of these words mean "to move fast," but there's a difference!

................... **Did You Know?** ....................

*Ran* and *run* are forms of the verb *to run.*

**Use *ran* alone.**

> I **ran** as fast as I could.
> My shadow **ran** behind me.

**Use *run* with *has* or *have*.**

> I **have run** beside a stream.
> The water **has run** along with me.

## Show What You Know

**Write *ran* or *run* in each blank.**

1. The ice cream has _____ down the cone.

2. The water _____ down the hill.

3. The spilled milk _____ off the table.

4. The fan has _____ all day.

Score: _____     Total Possible: 4

# Proofread

**There are four mistakes in this story. Draw a line through each incorrect word. Write the correct word above it.**

**Example:** The kitten has ~~ran~~ after the toy.
<sup>run</sup> appears above "ran"

Chris run to the basketball hoop. Delia and Tomas ran to block her.

Have they ran fast enough? No, Chris throws the ball. It goes through

the hoop. Chris sits down to rest. Tisha has ran onto the court. She will

play for Chris. She has ran all day before. She will not get tired.

# Practice

**Think about animals, people, and things that run. Write one sentence using *ran*. Write another sentence using *has run* or *have run*.**

1. _____

_____

_____

2. _____

# Tips for Your Own Writing: Proofreading ..............

Next time you write about something that runs, look for *ran, has run,* and *have run.* Have you used them correctly?

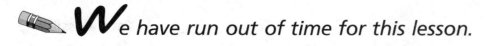 *e have run out of time for this lesson.*

# 32 Usage: Verbs–Did, Done

*D*o you know how to use did *and* done?

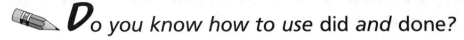

## .................... Did You Know? ....................

***Did*** **and** ***done*** **are forms of the verb** ***to do.***

**Use** ***did*** **alone.**

> I **did** my homework.
> Pat **did** his, too.

**Use** ***done*** **with** ***has*** **or** ***have.***

> I **have done** all my homework.
> Pat **has done** his, too.

# Show What You Know

**Read the poem below. If the underlined word is used incorrectly, draw a line through it and write the correct word above it.**

Once there was a strange kingdom

With a king who <u>did</u> the farming,
 1

A queen who <u>done</u> the banking,
 2

A prince who <u>did</u> the armor-making,
 3

A princess who <u>done</u> the fishing,
 4

And a sailor who has <u>did</u> the sewing.
 5

Score: _____     Total Possible: 3

**68**

# Proofread

**This report has three mistakes. Draw a line through each incorrect word. Write the correct word above it.**

**Example:** We ~~done~~ a good job.
<small>did</small>

Last month, Nature Club members done a good thing. They cleaned

up the playground. Ten members have did a big poster about recycling.

They done a great job. They will hang the poster in the gym.

# Practice

**Think about a chore you or your friends have done. Write two sentences about it. Be sure to use _did_, _have done_, or _has done_ in each sentence.**

1. _____

   _____

   _____

2. _____

# Tips for Your Own Writing: Proofreading ..............

The next time you want to write _did_ or _done_, make sure _did_ is alone. Make sure _done_ is with _has_ or _have_.

✎ **W**hat have you (did, <u>done</u>) to make your writing better?

# 33 Review: Verbs

**A.** **Read the sentences below. If the underlined word is incorrect, draw a line through it and write the correct word above it.**

Jeff has <u>ran</u> down the stairs. His dog and cat <u>ran</u> after him. Why
　　　　1　　　　　　　　　　　　　　　　　　2

have they all <u>ran</u> so fast? Jeff has <u>run</u> to catch the bus. The dog and cat
　　　　　3　　　　　　　　　　　　4

have <u>ran</u> to catch Jeff.
　　　5

Score: _____　　Total Possible: 3

**B.** **Read the poem below. Write *did* or *done* in each blank.**

_____ you see the sun get ready for bed?
　　　1

_____ you see the moon sing the sun to sleep?
　　　2

My eyes _____ not close all night.
　　　　　　　3

But they have _____ that now.
　　　　　　　　　4

Score: _____　　Total Possible: 4

**C. Read this paragraph. Look for *ran* and *run*. If the word is used incorrectly, draw a line through it. Write the correct word above it. There are five mistakes.**

Li and Josh and Ben have ran  a race. They run  fast. Josh and Li ran

all the way to the gate and back. Ben did not know how far to go. He

has ran  to the gate. He has not ran  back. Now they will have to ran  the

race again.                                         Score: _____     Total Possible: 5

**D. Read these sentences. Write the correct word in each blank.**

**1.** Do you know what Ann has _____? **(did, done)**

**2.** She has _____ into the bushes with her bike. **(ran, run)**

**3.** April _____ into the same bushes with her skates. **(ran, run)**

**4.** The bushes _____ not know what to do. **(did, done)**

**5.** They have _____ their best to stay away from girls. **(did, done)**

Score: _____     Total Possible: 5

REVIEW SCORE: _____     REVIEW TOTAL: 17

# 34 Usage: Verbs—Went, Gone

*Do you know when to use each of these words?*

## .................... Did You Know? ..........

**Went** and *gone* are forms of the verb *to go.*

**Use *went* alone.**

Rosa **went** to the snake house.

**Use *gone* with *has* or *have.***

Erik **has gone** to the monkey house.

## Show What You Know

**Read the sentences below. Fill in each blank with *went* or *gone.***

Mr. Mingle _____ to the zoo. His students have _____
1                                                   2

with him. First they _____ to see the lions. One lion roared at
3

them. Then two owls hooted. Ryan _____ to see them. The owl he
4

found was two feet tall! Now the owl has _____ to sleep.
5

Score: _____     **Total Possible: 5**

# Proofread

**This note has four mistakes. Draw a line through each incorrect word. Write the correct word above it.**

**Example:** My sister has ~~went~~ to school.
<sup>gone</sup>

Dad and I went to my soccer game. John has went with us. We

have went to pick up Julie and Justin. Jeremy has not went with us. He

and Jeff gone to watch a woman juggle. Aunt Judy went with them.

# Practice

**Write two sentences about a time you went somewhere. Be sure to use *went, has gone,* or *have gone* in each sentence.**

1. _____

_____

2. _____

# Tips for Your Own Writing: Proofreading .............

Read something you have written. Look for the verbs *went* and *gone.*
Make sure you have used *went* by itself and *gone* with *has* or *have.*

 **Y**ou have (*went*, <u>*gone*</u>) *through this lesson.*

# 35 Usage: Verbs–Saw, Seen

*See if you can spot the difference between saw and seen.*

## ....................... Did You Know? .........

**Saw** and **seen** are forms of the verb **to see.**

**Use saw alone.**

I **saw** a black and white whale.

**Use seen with has or have.**

Beth **has seen** a big, blue whale.

## Show What You Know

**Read the story below. Fill in each blank with *saw* or *seen*.**

José and Eva have _____ a fire truck. It raced down the
<sub>1</sub>

street. They have _____ its red and white lights flash. They stop.
<sub>2</sub>

Drivers also _____ the truck. They stop their cars. A boy on a
<sub>3</sub>

bicycle has _____ everyone stop. He stops. José and Eva
<sub>4</sub>

_____ everyone but the fire truck stop.
<sub>5</sub>

Score: _____    Total Possible: 5

74

# Proofread

**This postcard has two mistakes. Draw a line through each incorrect word. Write the correct word above it.**

**Example:** We ~~seen~~ Aunt Della at the store.
saw

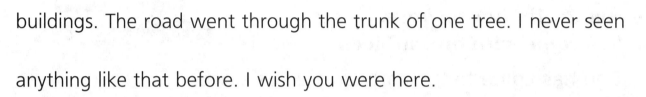

We are having fun on our trip. I seen

giant sequoia trees. They are taller than

buildings. The road went through the trunk of one tree. I never seen

anything like that before. I wish you were here.

# Practice

**Write two sentences about something you have seen. Remember to use *saw*, *have seen*, or *has seen* in each sentence.**

1. _____

_____

_____

2. _____

# Tips for Your Own Writing: Proofreading ..............

Remember that *saw* and *seen* tell about the past. Use *saw* alone. Use *seen* with *has* or *have*.

*N*ow you have (saw, <u>seen</u>) how to use these words.

# 36 Usage: Verbs—Came, Come

*This lesson has come along at just the right time.*

························· **Did You Know?** ·····················

***Came*** and ***come*** are forms of the verb *to come.*

Use ***came*** alone.

> The children **came** to Ling's party.

Use ***come*** with *has* or *have.*
Use ***has come*** with one subject.

> Deb **has come** to the party dressed as a bee.

Use ***have come*** when you talk about more than one subject.

> Rosa and Jake **have come** dressed like crayons.

··············································

## Show What You Know

**Everything lives somewhere. The sentences below match animals with their homes. Fill in each blank with *came* or *come*.**

1. The busy bee _____ to the hive.

2. The noisy blue jay _____ to the nest.

3. The black bear has _____ to the cave.

Score: _____    Total Possible: 3

# Proofread

**There are three mistakes in this note. Draw a line through each incorrect word. Write the correct word above it.**

**Example:** She ~~come~~ <sup>came</sup> on time.

I'm glad you come to my party. You have always came in neat

costumes. I liked your funny scarecrow costume. I did not know your

crow come from a store. My cat is sorry he tried to

eat your crow!

# Practice

**Choose two words from the list below and write two sentences. Be sure to use *came*, *has come*, or *have come* in each sentence.**

| | | | | |
|---|---|---|---|---|
| movie theater | park | pool | grocery store | circus |
| friend's house | dentist | library | post office | pet store |

1. _____

_____

2. _____

# Tips for Your Own Writing: Proofreading ..............

Next time you write about a trip, look for the words *came* and *come*.
Make sure you have used *came* by itself and *come* with *has* or *have*.

 **T**his lesson has come to an end.

# 37 Review: Verbs

**A. Read the story below. Write *came* or *come* in each blank.**

The sea _____ to the beach.
1

It has _____ as far as it can reach.
2

Do you think it _____ to find a shell?
3

Maybe it has _____ with a tale to tell.
4

Score: _____     **Total Possible: 4**

**B. Read the story below. Write *saw* or *seen* in each blank.**

I went to the circus. I _____ a clown riding a mule. Then I
1

noticed something funny. I _____ two monkeys riding on the
2

clown. I have not _____ that before! Then I _____ four
3      4

doves riding on the monkeys. Were eight fleas riding on the doves?

Score: _____     **Total Possible: 4**

**C. Read the story below. Write *went* or *gone* in each blank.**

Amy has _____ to the park. She wants to climb the rock

                  1

mountain. Rob and Pete _____ with her. They have _____

                  2                                     3

to slide and swing. Do you think they _____ the short way? They

                                    4

would have had to walk through the mud.

Score: _____    Total Possible: 4

**D. Look at the words in each column. Draw a line between pairs that make sense. Use each pair only once.**

Ted and Liz have                          went to see the movie star.

My brother                                 ran to get the mail.

Tess                                       gone to feed the ducks.

Gilbert has                                come home early today.

Morgan                                 run a hundred miles.

I think Carmen has                    came to the park with us.

Score: _____    Total Possible: 6

REVIEW SCORE: _____    REVIEW TOTAL: 18

# 38 Usage: Adjectives That Compare

*These words can add some sparkle to your writing.*

## ·················· Did You Know? ····················

We can use words to describe and compare things. Add *-er* to an adjective when you compare two things. Add *-est* when you compare three or more things.

That airplane is **fast.**
This airplane is **faster** than that one.
This airplane is the **fastest** of all.

## Show What You Know

**This chart is not complete. Fill in the empty boxes with the correct word.**

| | | |
|---|---|---|
| short | shorter | shortest |
| large | | largest |
| | brighter | |
| long | longer | |
| | | highest |

Score: _____     **Total Possible: 6**

# Proofread

**This report has four mistakes. Draw a line through each incorrect word. Write the correct word above it.**

**Example:** Ben is ~~shortest~~ shorter than Tim.

A gorilla is big. A chimp is smallest than a gorilla. A tiger is strong than a lion. Did you know that tigers do not live in Africa? A man smart than my brother told me that. He also told me that a cheetah is the faster animal of all.

# Practice

**Use the words from the box on page 80 to compare something. Write two sentences. Be sure to write whole sentences, like this one.**

Becky's bike is **taller** than Seth's. My bike is the **tallest** one at the bike rack.

1. _____

2. _____

# Tips for Your Own Writing: Proofreading ...............

Next time you compare something, make sure you use -er words to talk about two things. Use -est words to talk about more than two.

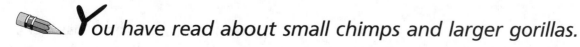 *You have read about small chimps and larger gorillas.*

# 39 Usage: Homophones–To/Too/Two

*T*his lesson will help you keep these three little words straight.

.................... **Did You Know?** ....................

Some words sound alike even when they mean different things and have different spellings.

The word *to* has two meanings. It can mean "toward." *To* is also used before a verb.

> I found a penny when I walked **to** the store.
> I want **to** read that book.

The word *too* has two meanings. It can mean "also." *Too* can also be used to mean "very" or "more than enough."

> Ike found a penny, **too**.
> I am **too** tired to watch the movie.

The word *two* means the number 2.

> Paul found **two** pennies.

## Show What You Know

**Read the paragraph below. Fill in each blank with *to, too,* or *two.***

My brother is learning _____ juggle. He started with

_____ balls. I asked him _____ teach me, _____.
　　2　　　　　　　　　　　　3　　　　　　　4

Score: _____　　　Total Possible: 4

# Proofread

**This note has four mistakes. Draw a line through each incorrect word. Write the correct word above it.**

**Example:** I'm not ~~to~~ <sup>too</sup> sleepy.

Julie asked me to come too her party. She is going two have to

cakes and too kinds of ice cream. Jill is coming, too. It will be so much

fun. I cannot wait to go.

# Practice

**Write two sentences. One should be about *two* of something. The other should tell about going to a place you like. Try to use *too* in one of the sentences, too!**

1. _____

_____

2. _____

# Tips for Your Own Writing: Proofreading ..............

Read a piece of your writing. Look for the words *to*, *too*, and *two*. Have you used *two* when you are talking about a number? Have you used *too* to mean "also," "very," or "more than enough"? Have you used *to* before verbs or to mean "toward"?

**Y**ou have had more than (to, too, <u>two</u>) chances (<u>to</u>, too, two) *use these same-sounding words.*

# 40 Review: Adjectives, Homophones

**A. Read the poem below. Write *to, too,* or *two* in each blank.**

This morning it started _____ rain.

The _____ of us were sad.

We couldn't go _____ our baseball game.

"That's _____ bad," said Dad.

Score: _____        Total Possible: 4

**B. Fill in the blanks to complete the chart.**

| | | |
|---|---|---|
| slow | | |
| fast | faster | |
| | darker | |
| little | | littlest |
| tall | | |
| | | shortest |

Score: _____        Total Possible: 10

**C. Finish the comparisons by writing the correct word in each blank.**

1. An eagle is _____ than a sparrow. **(big, bigger, biggest)**

2. A dinosaur might have been the _____ animal of all time. **(heavy, heavier, heaviest)**

3. A bus has _____ seats than a car. (large, larger, largest)

4. The night sky is _____ than the day sky. **(dark, darker, darkest)**

5. That is a _____ feather pillow. **(soft, softer, softest)**

6. This oak tree is the _____ one on my block. **(old, older, oldest)**

7. The ocean is _____ than the pool. **(cold, colder, coldest)**

8. Monday was _____. **(hot, hotter, hottest)**

Score: _____     Total Possible: 8

REVIEW SCORE: _____     REVIEW TOTAL: 22

# 41 Usage: Plurals That Add -s

*Changing a noun from one to more than one is easy!*

## Did You Know?

Nouns are words that name objects. You can make most nouns mean "more than one" by adding *-s* to the end of the word. This is called a plural noun.

one shoe     two shoe**s**
one balloon     five balloon**s**

## Show What You Know

**Write each word so that it means more than one.**

**1.** animal _____

**2.** sister _____

**3.** kitten _____

**4.** truck _____

**5.** backpack _____

**6.** bat _____

**7.** book _____

**8.** toy _____

**9.** dog _____

**10.** river _____

Score: _____     Total Possible: 10

# Proofread

**There are three mistakes in this invitation. Draw a line through each incorrect word. Write the correct word above it.**

**Example:** I saw two ~~dog~~. *(dogs)*

Please come to my party. We will play game and have fun. We will

eat hot dog, chip, and birthday cake. The party will

last two hours. Hope you can come!

# Practice

**Fill in the blanks to make a list about the picture. Use the words to write two sentences about the picture.**

one _____

two _____ with polka dots

three _____

four _____

1. _____

2. _____

# Tips for Your Own Writing: Proofreading ..............

When you write a word that means more than one, check to see that you have added -s.

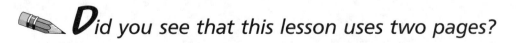 *id you see that this lesson uses two pages?*

# 42 Usage: Plurals That Add -es

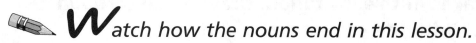 *Watch how the nouns end in this lesson.*

## Did You Know?

To make some nouns mean more than one, you add *-es*. Add *-es* to words ending in *sh, ch, x, s,* and *z*.

| | |
|---|---|
| one brush | two brush**es** |
| one dress | two dress**es** |

## Show What You Know

**Write each word so that it means more than one.**

**1.** brush  _____

**2.** ax  _____

**3.** box  _____

**4.** bench  _____

**5.** class  _____

**6.** dress  _____

**7.** flash  _____

**8.** lunch  _____

**9.** dish  _____

**10.** fox  _____

Score: _____    Total Possible: 10

# Proofread

**This poem has two mistakes. Can you fix them? Cross out each incorrect word. Write the correct word above it.**

**Example:** There are three ~~box~~ boxes on the table.

I was lunching one day up at Trish's

When an elf came and offered me wish.

I looked at my peas

Said "Thank you" and "Please,

Use my wishes to clean up these dish!"

# Practice

**Choose two words that mean more than one from the list on page 88. Use each word in a sentence.**

1. _____

_____

2. _____

# Tips for Your Own Writing: Proofreading ..............

Remember: When you want to make a word mean more than one, look at the end of the word. If it ends in *s, x, z, sh,* or *ch,* add *-es* to the end.

 *Do you need to wear glasses to do this lesson?*

# 43 Review: Plurals

**A. Add -s to make each word mean "more than one." Write the word on the line.**

**1.** ball _____

**2.** bat _____

**3.** shoe _____

**4.** glove _____

**5.** field _____

Score: _____     Total Possible: 5

**B. Add -es to make each word mean "more than one." Write the word on the line.**

**1.** brush _____

**2.** box _____

**3.** sash _____

**4.** mess _____

**5.** lunch _____

Score: _____     Total Possible: 5

**C. Fill in the blanks. Add _-s_ or _-es_ to the word in parentheses ( ).**

1. Aunt Min sent me a box of _____. **(paint)**

2. She also sent two new _____. **(brush)**

3. My brother got ten _____. **(marker)**

4. We have made a lot of _____. **(picture)**

5. We have made a lot of _____, too. **(mess)**

6. I am sending two _____ to Aunt Min. **(painting)**

7. One is a girl holding two _____ of flowers. **(bunch)**

8. One is a girl running the _____ on a baseball field. **(base)**

9. The paintings of the _____ are both of me. **(girl)**

10. I like to do a lot of _____. **(thing)**

Score: _____    Total Possible: 10

REVIEW SCORE: _____    REVIEW TOTAL: 20

# 44 Usage: Contractions

*This lesson is about taking shortcuts when you speak and write.*

····················· **Did You Know?** ·····················

Sometimes we put two words together to make one shorter word. The shorter word is called a contraction.

> is not—is**n't**       are not—are**n't**
> was not—was**n't**     were not—were**n't**

When we make contractions by using *not*, we leave out the *o* in *not* and put an apostrophe (') in its place.

## Show What You Know

**Write the contraction on the line.**

**1.** is not  _____

**3.** was not  _____

**2.** are not  _____

**4.** were not  _____

**Write the correct contraction in each sentence.**

**1.** Amy _____ going to the party. **(isn't, aren't)**

**2.** The boys _____ happy about the team. **(wasn't, weren't)**

Score: _____       Total Possible: 6

# Proofread

**Find the four mistakes in this paragraph. Draw a line through each incorrect word. Write the correct word above it.**

**Example:** They ~~arent~~ aren't here today.

The clouds were big yesterday. But they werent very fluffy. Bill

wasnot here to see them. Bill is here today, is'nt he? Are'nt he and Les

over by the fence? No, that's someone else.

# Practice

**Write one sentence about someone you know. Use *isn't* or *aren't*. Write another sentence about you or a friend. Use *wasn't* or *weren't*.**

**Examples:** My brother isn't tall.
I wasn't tired.

1. _____

2. _____

# Tips for Your Own Writing: Proofreading ..............

Look at a story you have written. Find the words *isn't, aren't, wasn't,* and *weren't*. Have you spelled them correctly? Is the apostrophe (') in the right place?

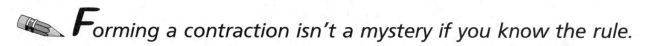*F*orming a contraction isn't a mystery if you know the rule.

# 45 Usage: Isn't, Aren't

*Here are two words you use every day. Do you use them correctly?*

.................... **Did You Know?** ....................

**Isn't** and *aren't* are contractions. Use *isn't* when you talk about one.

Rachel **isn't** eating her peas.

**Use *aren't* when you talk about more than one.**

Sue and Ann **aren't** eating their peas, either.

## Show What You Know

**Read the story below. Fill in the blanks with *isn't* or *aren't*.**

My grandmother _____ like most grandmothers. My brother
1

and I _____ allowed to eat cookies before supper. We
2

_____ allowed to stay up late. But my grandmother takes me to
3

the park. She lets me play on the really big slide. She _____
4

supposed to do that. _____ my grandmother a lot of fun?
5

Score: _____     Total Possible: 5

# Proofread

**Read Jill's report about two animals she saw at the zoo. Draw a line through each incorrect word. Write the correct word above it. There are three mistakes.**

**Example:** That book ~~aren't~~ isn't about animals.

Lions and tigers isn't the same. A lion's mane isnt on a tiger. A

tiger's stripes isn't on a lion. A lion is a cat, and a tiger is a cat. But a

tiger isn't a lion.

# Practice

**Write two sentences about something that was not done right. Use _isn't_ and _aren't_.**

**Examples:** My toast isn't dark.
My eggs aren't ready.

1. _____

_____

2. _____

# Tips for Your Own Writing: Proofreading ..............

When you write _isn't_ or _aren't,_ remember to put the apostrophe (') in the right place. Have you used _isn't_ to talk about one? Have you used _aren't_ to talk about more than one?

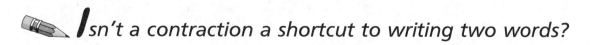 _Isn't a contraction a shortcut to writing two words?_

# 46 Usage: Wasn't, Weren't

*What is the difference between these words?*

························· **Did You Know?** ·······················

*Wasn't* and *weren't* are two more contractions.

**Use *wasn't* when you talk about one.**

Tom **wasn't** on the bus.

**Use *weren't* when you talk about more than one and with the word *you*.**

**Weren't** Lee and Min the last to get on?
You **weren't** the last one.

· · · · · · · · · · · · · · · · · · · · · · · · · · · · · · · · · · ·

# Show What You Know

**Read the story below. Write *wasn't* or *weren't* in the blanks.**

My brother Mike _____ eating his peas. He put them in
                        1

the flowerpot. Mom noticed. Peas _____ part of her ivy plant.
                                        2

Then Mike tried to make the dog eat his peas. The dog _____
                                                              3

happy. I hoped Mike's peas _____ about to land on my plate!
                                  4

Score: _____   **Total Possible: 4**

# Proofread

**This thank-you note has three mistakes. Draw a line through each incorrect word. Write the correct word above it.**

**Example:** You ~~wasn't~~ <sup>weren't</sup> late.

Dear Aunt Jo,

    Thank you for taking me to the circus. Weren't it fun? I weren't

really scared. I knew those two men weren't going to fall. You wasn't

scared, were you?

Love,

Ashley

# Practice

**Write two sentences. Use *wasn't* or *weren't* in each sentence.**
**Examples:** The pool wasn't open.
           The children weren't happy.

1. _____

2. _____

# Tips for Your Own Writing: Proofreading ..............

Check your writing for the words *wasn't* and *weren't*. Have you used *wasn't* to talk about one? Have you used *weren't* with the word *you* and to talk about more than one?

 (<u>*wasn't*</u>, *weren't*) finished using these contractions.

# 47 Review: Contractions

**A. Read the story below. Write *isn't* or *aren't* in each blank.**

My dog Bo _____ a collie.
1

He _____ a husky, either. My
2

father and mother _____ sure what he is. He likes to run. He
3

chases the ball I throw. He _____ ready to stop when I am.
4

Score: _____    Total Possible: 4

**B. Lucy wrote about "Jack and the Beanstalk." She could not remember when to use *wasn't* and *weren't.* Help her out. Write the correct word in each blank.**

Jack and his mom _____ rich. They needed to sell their
1

cow. Jack _____ supposed to trade the cow for three beans.
2

His mom _____ happy when he came home with beans.
3

_____ they surprised when a big beanstalk grew!
4

Score: _____    Total Possible: 4

**C. Read this story. Look for *isn't, aren't, wasn't,* and *weren't.* Find the six mistakes. Draw a line through each incorrect word. Write the correct word above it.**

The rabbits are'nt in the cage. Where did they go? I hope Nell is

giving them a bath. They werent clean enough. Aren't she supposed to

clean the cage, too? Yes, but aren't Patrick and Janice going to help?

They isn't home. This isno't fair. Oh, look! We have six clean rabbits. I

guess I will clean the cage. The rabbits isn't going to get dirty again.

Score: _____     Total Possible: 6

**D. Finish these sentences with *isn't* or *aren't.***

1. My name _____ Sal.

2. My eyes _____ blue.

3. My song _____ long.

4. My stories _____ true.

Score: _____     Total Possible: 4

REVIEW SCORE: _____     REVIEW TOTAL: 18

**99**

# 48 Usage: Adding -ed

*You can change the meaning of a verb by adding -ed.*

## .................. Did You Know? ..................

**To make most verbs tell about the past, you add *-ed* to the end of the word.**

want     want**ed**
lift      lift**ed**

**If the action word ends in *e*, add just *-d*.**

like     like**d**
use     use**d**

## Show What You Know

**Fill in the blanks with the verb that shows that the action happened in the past.**

**1.** Min _____ the ball to Lee. **(kick, kicked)**

**2.** Jeff _____ to play, too. **(want, wanted)**

**3.** Lee and Min _____ him over. **(call, called)**

**4.** Jeff _____ over. **(rush, rushed)**

**5.** They all _____ the ball. **(use, used)**

Score: _____     Total Possible: 5

# Proofread

**This story has six mistakes. Draw a line through each incorrect word. Write the correct word above it.**

**Example:** I ~~talk~~ to my friend last night.
*(talked written above talk)*

On Friday, Amy skate with Anna and April. They are good friends.

Amy ask Anna and April to skate next to her. They look like sisters. Amy

turned around and skate backwards. Anna twirl. April wanted to twirl.

She fell down instead. Amy help April get up.

# Practice

**Write two sentences about something you did this week. Use action words with *-ed* on the end.**

1. _____

2. _____

# Tips for Your Own Writing: Proofreading ..............

Next time you write about something that happened in the past, check your verbs. Have you spelled them correctly? Did you add *-ed*? If the word ended in *e*, did you add only the *-d*?

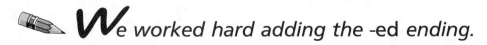

***We worked hard adding the -ed ending.***

# 49 Usage: Adding -s

✏ *Say this three times: She sells seashells.*

......................... **Did You Know?** .......................

**Action verbs that tell what one subject is doing end in *s*.**

She **runs.** He **runs.** It **runs.** The dog **barks.**

**Action verbs that tell what more than one subject is doing do not end in *s*.**

The dogs **bark.**

**Action verbs that tell about you, we, or they do not end in *s*, either.**

You **run.** We **run.** They **run.**

## Show What You Know

**Fill in the blanks with the correct form of the verb. Draw a circle around the person or thing the verb tells about.**

**1.** Jan _____ the ball. **(kick, kicks)**

**2.** The ball _____ into the bushes. **(roll, rolls)**

**3.** Ben _____ and tugs, but the ball is stuck. **(pull, pulls)**

**4.** Jan _____ on the ball until it pops free. **(tug, tugs)**

Score: _____    Total Possible: 8

# Proofread

**There are three mistakes in this report. Draw a line through each incorrect word. Write the correct word above it.**

**Example:** I ~~walks~~ to school.
(walk written above walks)

    I live in a noisy house. My brother yells. The dogs barks. The cat say

meow, meow, meow. Even the bird talk. She says "good morning" to me

every night.

# Practice

**Look at the picture. Write two sentences about what the children are doing. Use action words.**

1. _____

_____

_____

2. _____

# Tips for Your Own Writing: Proofreading ..............

Look at a piece of your writing. Check your action verbs. Do they end in -s when you talk about one person or thing? How do they end when you talk about more than one person or thing, or about you, we, or they?

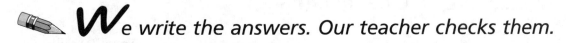 *We write the answers. Our teacher checks them.*

# 50 Review: Adding -ed/-s

**A. Fill in each blank. Show that the action has already happened.**

1. Last week, Ben _____ his drum. **(play)**

2. He _____ on it with sticks. **(bang)**

3. The neighbors _____ their ears. **(cover)**

4. Ben's mom _____ her door. **(close)**

Score: _____        Total Possible: 4

**B. Fill in each blank. Show that the action is happening right now.**

1. Roger _____ for his homework

   **(hunt)**

2. He _____ many things, but

   not that. **(see)**

3. His baseball bat _____ in the corner. **(sit)**

4. His hat _____ on the light. **(hang)**

Score: _____        Total Possible: 4

**C. Choose the correct form of the word. Write your answer in each blank.**

1. Cinderella _____ hard. **(work, works)**

2. She _____ dishes all day. **(clean, cleans)**

3. She _____ torn clothing late at night. **(sew, sews)**

4. The mice _____ Cinderella a little. **(help, helps)**

5. Her mean sisters _____ while she worked. **(plays, played)**

6. Cinderella _____ about the Prince's ball. **(think, thinks)**

Score: _____  Total Possible: 6

**D. This recipe tells how to make breakfast. Look at the underlined words. If the wrong verb is used, cross it out. Write the correct verb above it. There are five mistakes.**

First you <u>opens</u> the box. Then you <u>pours</u> out the cereal. Oops, I
         1                              2

forgot. You <u>need</u> a bowl. My mother <u>add</u> milk for me. I <u>spills</u> the milk
           3                              4                      5

when I pour it. Then I <u>eats</u> my breakfast.
                       6

Score: _____  Total Possible: 5

REVIEW SCORE: _____  REVIEW TOTAL: 19

**105**

# 51 Usage: Using *I*

✎ *Y*ou and I will learn about the word I.

## ............... Did You Know? ...................

When you talk about what you do or who you are, use the word *I*.

Always write *I* with a capital letter. *I* is a pronoun that is used as a subject.

I helped my mom today.

When you talk about yourself and someone else, speak of yourself last.

**Mom and I** planted flowers outside.

## Show What You Know

**Finish this story. Write *I* in the blanks. Then read each sentence to a friend.**

Mom asked me to show her how a robot acts. _____ marched
<sub>1</sub>

across the room. Then she asked me to work hard like a robot. _____
<sub>2</sub>

put my toys away. _____ also gave Mom my dirty shirts and socks.
<sub>3</sub>

_____ think Mom tricked me into cleaning my room!
<sub>4</sub>

Score: _____          Total Possible: 4

# Proofread

**This journal entry has three mistakes. Cross out each mistake.
Write the correct word or words above it.**

**Example:** Mom and ~~me~~ ate breakfast.

I and Dad were busy today. We worked outside. i pulled weeds and

planted flowers. Pam came over, too. Dad, Pam, and I watered the new

plants. Pam and I got dirty. i had lots of fun.

# Practice

**Write two sentences to tell about
something you and someone else did.**

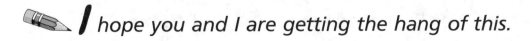

1. _____

_____

_____

2. _____

# Tips for Your Own Writing: Proofreading ..............

Look at a piece of writing in which you wrote about yourself. Circle
each *I*. Check to see whether you used it correctly.

*I hope you and I are getting the hang of this.*

# 52 Usage: Using *Me*

**K**nowing *when to use* me *can be a little tricky. This lesson will help.*

························· **Did You Know?** ·····················

Sometimes when you talk about yourself, you are not the main person the sentence is about. In this case, use the word *me*. *Me* is a pronoun, just like *I* is.

Barry walked with **me** to the pool.

When you talk about yourself and someone else, speak of yourself last.

Kandi came with **Barry and me.**

## Show What You Know

**Fill in each blank with the correct word or words.**

**1.** My brother Alex chased _____ through the house. **(I, me)**

**2.** He wanted _____ to take out the trash. **(I, me)**

**3.** Mom told _____ to stop running through the

house. **(me and Alex, Alex and me)**

**4.** So I ran outside, and Alex kept chasing _____! **(I, me)**

Score: _____    **Total Possible: 4**

# Proofread

**Find the four mistakes in this secret story. Draw a line through the incorrect word or words. Write the correct word or words above.**

**Example:** They were waiting for ~~me and Jilly~~. *(Jilly and me)*

    Dad and I have a secret. It is just between Dad and I. Dad told it to

I last night. He said he knew I would not tell. He said it was only for

me and him. Mom will want me and Dad to tell her. We cannot tell

Mom. The secret is about her birthday present.

# Practice

**Write two sentences about times when someone did something for you. Be sure to use *me* in each one.**
**Example:** My grandmother bought me a piece of apple pie.

1. _____

2. _____

# Tips for Your Own Writing: Proofreading .............

The next time you write about something that happened to you, use the word *me.* Use *I* when you are the one doing or being something. When you talk about yourself and a friend, speak of yourself last.

 *Sometimes I am confused when I talk about (I, __me__).*

# 53 Review: *I/Me*

**A. Read this paragraph. Write *I* or *me* in each blank.**

Pam and _____ went to the park. She and _____
            1                                              2

wanted to sled down the hill. Pam went first. She waited for _____
                                                                            3

at the bottom. She and _____ walked up the hill together. Next
                            4

time she and _____ rode together. The sled went very fast with
                5

Pam and _____ on it.
            6

Score: _____      **Total Possible: 6**

**B. Find the three mistakes in this story. Draw a line through the incorrect word. Write the correct word above it.**

**Example:** They called ~~I~~ on the phone. *(me)*

Me like to sleep with my teddy bear. He makes

me feel safe at night. The dark does not bother I

when Teddy is watching. I do not tell my

friends about my teddy. I think they might laugh. Mom

told I she used to sleep with a teddy bear.

Score: _____      **Total Possible: 3**

**C. Read each sentence. Choose the correct answer and write it in the blank.**

1. Both _____ wanted to go to the library.

   **(Dad and me, Dad and I)**

2. _____ needed a book for a book report. **(I, me)**

3. My little sister Becky wanted to come with _____ .

   **(me and Dad, Dad and me)**

4. _____ told Dad we should go to the children's

   section. **(Becky and I, I and Becky)**

5. I found a book _____ liked. **(I, me)**

6. Dad helped _____ check it out. **(I, me)**

7. _____ ran to the car with my book. **(I, me)**

8. Becky ran behind _____ . **(I, me)**

Score: _____    Total Possible: 8

REVIEW SCORE: _____    REVIEW TOTAL: 17

# 54 Grammar: Common Nouns

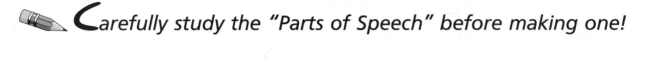

*Carefully study the "Parts of Speech" before making one!*

## ......................... Did You Know? .....................

**<u>Nouns</u> are parts of speech. Common nouns name any person, place, thing, or idea.**

Gabby is a crow who loves to shop. She sits on the telephone wire and "caws" the shopping channel. Gabby has bought so many things that her tree is too crowded.

# Show What You Know

**Look for the common nouns in this poem. Underline each one. You should find fourteen.**

Penny was a small pack rat,

Who collected many things

Like fuzzy hats, a thermostat,

Two bouncy springs, ten shiny rings,

A frying pan, an old tin can,

A ragged map, a bottle cap,

A Chinese fan, a little van,

A broken strap, and new mousetrap!

Score: _____     Total Possible: 14

# Practice

**Read the paragraph below. Write a common noun in each blank.**

I really wanted to have a _____<sub>1</sub>.

I asked my _____<sub>2</sub> whether I could

have one. I had to save money. Finally I went

to the _____<sub>3</sub> and bought a _____<sub>4</sub>. I fed it lots of

_____<sub>5</sub>, and my _____<sub>6</sub> began to grow and grow.

# Revise

**Write a sentence about another pet. Underline the common nouns.**

_____

_____

**Reread your sentence. Change some of the common nouns to make the sentence funny. Rewrite the sentence.**

_____

_____

# Tips for Your Own Writing: Proofreading ..............

Next time you write a letter, reread it. Can you find the common nouns? Ask someone to help you make sure you found all the common nouns.

 *A noun will tell you what all the fuss is about.*

# 55 Grammar: Common and Proper Nouns

✏️ *There is a proper way to name some parts of speech. My teacher, Mr. Gorman, told me that.*

························· **Did You Know?** ·····················

**A common noun** names any person, place, thing, or idea.

**A proper noun** names a special person, a special place, or a special thing. A proper noun begins with a capital letter.

Dr. Penn went to examine the piglets at Old McPorker's Farm. He prescribed "Babe's Sunscreen Oinkment" for their bad sunburn. They had been "bacon" in the sun!

## Show What You Know

**Read the poem. Circle every proper noun. You should find seven.**

At Zelda's Zany Zoo

The animals were sick.

Cameron Camel lost his hump.

Presley Python ate a stick.

Zelda quickly made a call

To Little Clinic in L.A.

Dr. Little flew out fast.

He came that very day.

Score: _____     Total Possible: 7

# Practice

**Read the paragraph below. Write a proper noun in each blank.**

My name is _____ . I am on a secret
              **1**

mission to find out why the children at _____
                                          **2**

School in _____ make animal sounds. First, I asked
            **3**

_____ , and he barked. Then I asked _____ , and the
   **4**                                      **5**

mystery was solved. They all want to be teacher's pet!

# Revise

**Write one sentence that tells about a special person or place. Underline the proper noun.**

_____

_____

_____

**Think of one more proper noun to add to your sentence. Rewrite the sentence.**

_____

_____

_____

# Tips for Your Own Writing: Proofreading .............

Look at two practice sentences you have written for another lesson. Can you find the proper nouns?

*Some nouns are prim and proper. Mr. Grim says, "Treat proper nouns properly!"*

# 56 Grammar: Pronouns

✏️ *Talk about yourself. Did you use the word* I *to refer to yourself? Great! Then you already know something about pronouns.*

## Did You Know?

**Pronouns** take the place of nouns. These replacements must be chosen carefully! Some pronouns you might use are *I, me, you, he, him, she, her, it, we, us, they, them, my, mine, your, his, her, hers, its, ours,* and *their.*

What should a little boy say when <u>he</u> meets a three-headed monster?
"Hello. How are <u>you</u>? Hello. How are <u>you</u>? Hello. How are <u>you</u>?"

## Show What You Know

**Read the riddles below. Circle every pronoun. You will circle six. Look at the list in *Did You Know?* if you need some help.**

Little Monster, where did you get that wild doll?

I made it with my own six little hands!

Why did the monster want to become a photographer?

She loved being in dark rooms.

Why did the monster cross the road?

He wanted to eat the chicken!

Score: _____     Total Possible: 6

# Practice

**Read the paragraph below. Write the correct pronoun in each blank.**

Mrs. Monster told the twins to clean

_____

their room. _____ did not feel like
1

cleaning. _____ went outside and quickly came back.
2

"Where did _____ go?" asked their mother.
3

"_____ were going to run away, but _____
4                                              5

remembered that you won't let us," one monster answered.

# Revise

**Write a sentence about a funny monster.**

_____

_____

_____

**Replace the noun with a pronoun.**

_____

_____

_____

# Tips for Your Own Writing: Proofreading ...............

Read a story you have written. Look for pronouns. Did you use pronouns in place of nouns to make the sentences sound better?

*P**ronouns are exactly like substitute teachers. They are not exactly the same as the original, but they are important, too!*

# 57 Grammar: Verbs

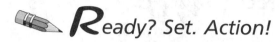 *R*eady? Set. Action!

················· **Did You Know?** ·····················

**Verbs** are parts of speech that can show action. They tell what is happening. Without action verbs, nothing would get done!

Sherman slowly <u>climbed</u> up the stairs. He <u>dragged</u> his feet as he <u>walked</u> to the edge. He <u>bounced</u> up and down.

"Sherman, <u>dive</u> now! The pool just <u>closed</u>!" <u>yelled</u> his dad.

·········································

# Show What You Know

**Read the poem below about a vacation. Circle eight action verbs.**

We drove along eight hours.

Will and I slept for five.

We read the other three hours.

And then at last we arrived.

We parked close to our cabin.

We carried in all our things.

Then we swam a little while.

And later we played on the swings.

Score: _____    **Total Possible: 8**

# Practice

**Read the paragraph below about an amusement park. Write an action verb in each blank.**

My family and I _____ the Tipsy
**1**

Turvy Amusement Park. We _____
**2**

around in circles on our first ride. Then we

_____ the tallest roller coaster. It slowly _____ up the
**3** **4**

hills and then quickly _____ down them.
**5**

# Revise

**Write a sentence that tells what might happen at the amusement park next. Underline your action verb.**

_____

_____

**Reread your sentence. Substitute a new action verb for the original verb. Rewrite the sentence. Underline the new action verb.**

_____

_____

# Tips for Your Own Writing: Revising .................

Look at two sentences you have written for another lesson. Circle your verbs. Can you think of other verbs you could use?

*Exercise good judgment in writing. Choose great action verbs!*

# 58 Review: Nouns, Pronouns, Verbs

**A. Read the paragraph. Write a common noun in each blank.**

Mom said that it was time to clean

my _____. I had not done this for
<br>1

two _____, so I did not know what I would find. First, I looked
<br>2

under my _____. I was surprised to see an ugly _____!
<br>3      4

After I moved the _____, I found an angry _____!
<br>5      6

Maybe I should clean my _____ more often.
<br>7

Score: _____      **Total Possible: 7**

**B. Read the story below. Circle the proper nouns. There are seven proper nouns.**

Tommy Twiddle and his sister Tess Twiddle did not know what to do.

Their favorite movie theater, Crazy Cartoons, was closed. They went to the

Play Until Dark Park, but it was closed. Finally, Tommy and Tess rode their

bikes to the Ready to Read Library. The bike rack was full. Everyone else

was looking for something to do, too!

Score: _____      **Total Possible: 7**

**C. Read the story below. Underline the thirteen pronouns. Look at *Did You Know?* on page 116 if you need help remembering pronouns.**

The knight was upset. He did not know what to do. The king and queen commanded him to find a dragon. They wanted to put it in the Royal Zoo. The poor knight knew that no dragons existed. They had not lived for many years. He sadly sat down on a rock.

Hours passed. An idea came to him when a dragonfly landed next to him. He picked it up and brought it to the king and queen. They were satisfied and happy. They had their dragon at last!

Score: _____      Total Possible: 13

**D. Read the sentences. Draw a circle around each action verb.**

**1.** Dr. Brainwave made a machine.

**2.** He walked inside.

**3.** What happened to the doctor?

**4.** He felt his head spinning!

**5.** His tummy turned flip-flops!

**6.** The doctor broke the machine.

Score: _____      Total Possible: 6

REVIEW SCORE: _____      REVIEW TOTAL: 33

# 59 Grammar: Adjectives

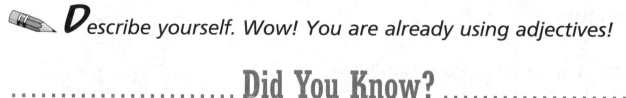

*Describe yourself. Wow! You are already using adjectives!*

## ..................... Did You Know? .....................

**Adjectives** describe nouns and pronouns. They are parts of speech that help paint a picture in your mind.

The <u>young</u>, <u>female</u> magician wears a <u>tall</u>, <u>red</u>, <u>polka-dotted</u> hat. She is standing on a <u>big</u> stage. The room is <u>dark</u>.

**An adjective can fit in the blanks in this sentence: The _____ dog is very _____.**

# Show What You Know

**Read the poem below. Circle eleven adjectives. If you want to test a word, use the last sentence from *Did You Know?*.**

Madge was a good magician.

She did amazing tricks.

She changed the small, blue eggs

Into little, purple chicks!

Madge put her magic wand

On a funny, yellow flower.

It changed into a green weed.

It grew taller by the hour!

Score: _____          **Total Possible: 11**

# Practice

**Read the paragraph below. Write different adjectives in each blank.**

Maybe I can become a _____
1

magician. I will need a _____ hat and a
2

_____ wand. I will wear a _____
3                                                    4

cape. After I say _____ words, I will make a _____
5                                                                        6

rabbit appear. I will even make my _____ homework disappear.
7

# Revise

**Write one sentence about a magic trick you could perform if you were a magician. Be sure to use at least one adjective.**

_____

_____

**Reread your sentence. Can you think of another adjective to add? Now rewrite the sentence with the new adjective.**

_____

_____

# Tips for Your Own Writing: Revising ..................

Look at a story you have written. Can you make your sentences say more by adding adjectives?

*Adjectives spark your imagination! They can change words into a magical picture in your mind!*

# 60 Grammar: Adverbs

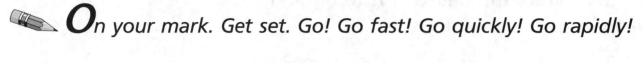 *On your mark. Get set. Go! Go fast! Go quickly! Go rapidly!*

## ..................... Did You Know? ....................

Adverbs are parts of speech that describe verbs. They help you "see" the action more clearly. Adverbs often answer the questions "How?" or "Where?". Find your verb, then ask "How?" or "Where?".

The alligator is diving into the pool.
The alligator is diving <u>down</u> into the pool.
Where is the alligator diving? Down!

The rooster crowed.
The rooster crowed <u>boldly</u>.
How did the rooster crow? Boldly.

## Show What You Know

**Read the sentences. Circle every adverb. There are five adverbs.**

1. The elephant pedaled slowly on the exercise bike.

2. The wolves quickly passed the football.

3. The monkey swung the bat evenly with its tail.

4. The crocodile fished silently without getting a bite.

5. The fish giggled noisily when the fisherman went home with nothing.

Score: _____    Total Possible: 5

# Practice

**Read the paragraph below. Write different adverbs in each blank.**

The animals were competing _____ in
1

track-and-field events. The kangaroo hopped

_____ over the high-jump pole. The cheetah
2

raced _____ to win the sprint. The turtle moved _____
3                                                          4

in the marathon. The frog jumped _____ in the long jump.
5

# Revise

**Write one sentence about another sport an animal might do.**

_____

_____

**Reread your sentence. Look at your verb and ask "How?" and "Where?" Rewrite your sentence with the adverb.**

_____

_____

# Tips for Your Own Writing: Proofreading ..............

Next time you write a letter about something you did, remember to use adverbs. They will help your reader picture what you did.

*Adverbs, like adjectives, trigger your imagination! Adverbs help you see vividly what is happening!*

# 61 Review: Adjectives, Adverbs

**A. Underline seventeen adjectives in the poem below.**

Biscuit was a happy dog.

She had a lovely home.

It had blue shingles on the roof

and pink pillows made of foam.

Bonesy lived a busy life.

He loved his nice, large farm.

He didn't have a small, snug bed

but had a warm, safe barn.

Biscuit loved the short, green grass

and white fences all around.

Bonesy loved the tall, brown wheat

with long rows for racing down.

Score: _____     Total Possible: 17

**B. Write a different adjective in each blank.**

The photographer took _____ pictures of my class. Sammy
    1

smiled and showed his _____ teeth. Tammy was proud of her
    2

_____ dress. Jimmy wore a _____ tie with his
    3                              4

_____ suit. This class has class!
    5

Score: _____     Total Possible: 5

**C. Draw a circle around the adverbs. There are five adverbs.**

My baby brother Brian cried loudly all night. I tossed quietly in my bed. I quickly pulled the covers over my head. I heard Mother singing softly to Brian. I hardly slept.

Score: _____     Total Possible: 5

**D. Have you ever had to get up early to do something? The person in this story is having a hard time getting up. Add adverbs to make the story easier to imagine.**

I did not hear the alarm ringing _____. I slept
                                              1

_____ in bed. Mom yelled _____ to wake me. First, I
         2                                        3

_____ opened my eyes. Then, I _____ climbed out of
         4                                        5

bed. I _____ got dressed. I _____ ate breakfast and
              6                              7

_____ brushed my teeth. I was finally ready to go fishing with
         8

my grandpa.

Score: _____     Total Possible: 8

REVIEW SCORE: _____     REVIEW TOTAL: 35

# 62 Grammar: Statements

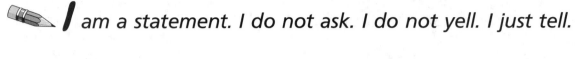 *I am a statement. I do not ask. I do not yell. I just tell.*

## ...................... Did You Know? ......................

**A <u>statement</u> is a sentence that tells something. Its first word begins with a capital letter. The sentence ends with a period.**

The old robot is rusty.
The lights are not so perky.
The gears are really dusty.
The arms and legs are jerky.

The new robot is smart.
It is twice the old one's size.
It can see in darkest dark.
It has brighter, shiny eyes.

# Show What You Know

**Read the paragraph below. Begin the first word of the nine statements with a capital letter. Put a period at the end of each one. Draw a circle around each period.**

poor Robby Robot had a bad day  he swallowed a yo-yo  he thought

that a computer disk was a Frisbee  he threw the disk out the window

Robby heard a funny joke  he laughed his head off  Robby went to bed

he could not fall asleep  he could not close his eyes

Score: _____    **Total Possible: 16**

# Practice

**Write two statements about a robot you would like to have.**

1. _____

2. _____

# Revise

**Can you add more information to your statements? Think about the lessons you have had on adjectives and adverbs. Add this information to your statements.**

1. _____

2. _____

**Reread your new statements. Do they sound more interesting than the first statements?**

# Tips for Your Own Writing: Proofreading .............

Look at **Practice** in another lesson. Did you write any statements? If you did, read your statements aloud to a friend.

*When you make a statement, you "tell it like it is."*

# 63 Grammar: Questions

*All questions need me. What am I? I am a question mark.*

## ·············· Did You Know? ·····················

A **question** is a sentence that asks something. Its first word begins with a capital letter. The sentence ends with a question mark.

"**W**hat will I be when I grow up**?**"
"Taller."

·······················································

# Show What You Know

**Read the poem below. Put a question mark at the end of six sentences that ask questions.**

My class went on a boating trip.

We sailed into a stream.

Watch those beavers take a dip.

Are they a swimming team.

Our teacher said she saw a fish.

Was that a flash of gold.

Quickly we will make a wish.

Is it a magic toad.

The current took us out to sea.

What is before our eyes.

Is it a dolphin swimming free.

He sees us. Down he dives.

We must go back before too long.

Look there. Is that a shark.

Teacher says we could be wrong.

We are looking in the dark.

Score: _____     Total Possible: 6

# Practice

**Write two questions you would ask to learn more about something that lives in the water.**

1. _____

2. _____

# Revise

**Rewrite one of your questions. Add more words to change the question a little.**

_____

_____

# Tips for Your Own Writing: Proofreading ..............

Look at a piece of writing you have done. Did you write any questions? Make sure you began each question with a capital letter and ended with a question mark.

*How will you ever learn the answers if you do not ask questions?*

# 64 Grammar: Exclamations

*Take advantage of an exclamation! Show the excitement when you write!*

...................... **Did You Know?** ......................

**An** <u>**exclamation**</u> **is a sentence that shows surprise or excitement. Its first word begins with a capital letter. The sentence ends with an exclamation point.**

The octopus wants to give me a big hug**!**
It's like having four mothers**!**

..............................................................

# Show What You Know

**Read the poem below. Put an exclamation point at the end of three sentences that could show surprise or excitement.**

I was in the shallow water.

A fish came swimming by.

Soon the fish had disappeared.

A shark was near. Oh, my.

He came close to show his teeth.

They were sharp and very white.

He opened up his big, big mouth.

But there was not a thing to bite.

I swam as fast as I knew how.

I was safe upon the path.

Then my mom called out to me,

"Are you finished with your bath?"

Score: _____    **Total Possible: 3**

# Practice

**Write two exciting sentences about swimming in the water. Be sure to end each with an exclamation point.**

1. _____

2. _____

# Revise

**Rewrite one of your exclamation sentences. Add new words to make the sentence even more exciting.**

_____

**Read your new exclamation. Does it sound more exciting than the first time you wrote it?**

# Tips for Your Own Writing: Proofreading ..............

Next time you want to share your excitement in your writing, remember to use an exclamation point.

*Exclamations are like dynamite. They can make small statements explode with excitement!*

# 65 Grammar: Commands

✎*A command is a sentence with power. "Do something now!" it says.*

······················· **Did You Know?** ·····················

**A command is a sentence that orders. Its first word begins with a capital letter. The sentence ends with a period or an exclamation point.**

Once there was a mean queen bee.
She ordered her workers around:
"**G**et me my honeycomb crown**!**
**F**ind flowers that are hard to see**!**"

···························································

## Show What You Know

**Read the conversation below. Put an exclamation point at the end of two sentences that are strong commands.**

The Queen Bee commanded, "Everyone, now get out your books.

Open your books to page 83. Begin studying the lesson. Then, write the

words on paper."

"Why do we have to practice every day?" asked a little bee quietly.

The Queen Bee answered, "We are the proud Spelling Bees. Now

get back to work."

Score: _____     Total Possible: 2

# Practice

Write two command sentences that a queen or a
king might say.

1. _____

2. _____

# Revise

Turn one of the commands into a person's spoken command. Tell
who is saying the command, and be sure to use quotation marks.

_____

Read your new command aloud. How do you say the command to
show the strength of the command?

# Tips for Your Own Writing: Proofreading ..............

Next time you write a story, remember to use commands. Strong
commands work well if you want to show that someone is powerful.

*Let a strong command be noticed! Use an exclamation point!*

# 66 Review: Sentences

**A. Read the story below carefully. Underline five sentences that are statements. Draw a circle around two questions. Draw two lines under one exclamation. Draw a box around one command. Then add the proper end marks.**

Did anyone hear the story about the old bear who lives in this forest

People say that he loved a girl bear named Honey One day Honey

vanished The old bear was very sad What do you think happened to

Honey No one knows for sure, but the old bear blamed the campers

Now at night he visits the camps and looks for Honey Yikes Be careful

tonight

Score: _____    Total Possible: 18

**B. Read the poem below. Put a period after six statements. Put a question mark after one question. Put an exclamation point after one exciting statement.**

I was building a snowman in my yard

Finding the snow was not too hard

A big, big snowstorm came last night

Everything here was covered in white

My small snowball began to roll

Quickly it went out of control

It began rolling down the big, big hill

Would it finally stop in Louisville

Score: _____    Total Possible: 8

**C. Read each sentence below. Decide whether it is a question, an exclamation, a command, or a statement. Circle the correct answer.**

**1.** Take your sister to the park!

    **Statement**        **Question**        **Exclamation**        **Command**

**2.** I think a monster lives under my bed and messes up my room.

    **Statement**        **Question**        **Exclamation**        **Command**

**3.** A green space creature ate my homework!

    **Statement**        **Question**        **Exclamation**        **Command**

**4.** Did you see the dolphin leap out of the water?

    **Statement**        **Question**        **Exclamation**        **Command**

**5.** I never wear a raincoat when it rains.

    **Statement**        **Question**        **Exclamation**        **Command**

**6.** Follow me!

    **Statement**        **Question**        **Exclamation**        **Command**

**7.** Do ostriches really bury their heads in the sand?

    **Statement**        **Question**        **Exclamation**        **Command**

**8.** That gorilla stole my banana!

    **Statement**        **Question**        **Exclamation**        **Command**

Score: _____        **Total Possible: 8**

**REVIEW SCORE:** _____        **REVIEW TOTAL: 34**

# 67 Grammar: Combining Sentences— Nouns

✏️ *Sometimes my friend and I use the "buddy system" when writing sentences. It can be twice as nice to do something together. Some sentences are better if they are put together.*

## ·················· Did You Know? ··················

**Some sentences tell about more than one subject. The word *and* joins the two subjects.**

Seals eat fish. People eat fish.
Seals **and** people eat fish.
Penguins wear dark suits. Business people
    wear dark suits.
Penguins **and** business people wear dark suits.

## Show What You Know

**Read each sentence below. Circle all of the subjects and the *and* that joins them.**

**1.** Leopards and sick children may see spots before their eyes.

**2.** Kangaroos and rich ladies have fur coats with big pockets.

**3.** Elephants and airport visitors have big trunks.

**4.** Rabbits and children can do the Bunny Hop.

**5.** Snakes and dieters bring their scales everywhere.

Score: _____        Total Possible: 5

# Practice

**Read each set of sentences below. Combine each set into one sentence. Look at *Did You Know?* to see how.**

**1.** Bears give big hugs. Dads give big hugs.

_____

- - - - - - - - - - - - - - - - - - - - - - - - -

_____

**2.** Frogs try to catch flies. Baseball players try to catch flies.

_____

- - - - - - - - - - - - - - - - - - - - - - - - -

_____

**3.** Parrots love to talk. Teenagers love to talk.

_____

- - - - - - - - - - - - - - - - - - - - - - - - -

_____

# Revise

**Look at your sentences. Think of another animal that shares some of the traits described. Choose one sentence. Rewrite the sentence changing the original animal.**

_____

- - - - - - - - - - - - - - - - - - - - - - - - -

_____

# Tips for Your Own Writing: Revising ..................

Look at a story you have written. Can you find places where two sentences talk about two people doing the same thing? Combine such sentences into one. Remember to use *and*.

*Sometimes more than one person or thing does the same thing in a sentence.*

# 68 Grammar: Combining Sentences– Verbs

✏️ *Pat your nose with one hand. Rub your tummy with the other. Pat your nose and rub your tummy at the same time! Sometimes we like to do more than one thing.*

## ........................ Did You Know? ....................

**A subject can do more than one thing in a sentence. When this is true, the sentence has more than one verb. The word *and* joins these verbs.**

Little Benny <u>jumps</u> in mud puddles. Little Benny <u>gets</u> me wet.

Little Benny <u>jumps</u> in mud puddles **and** <u>gets</u> me wet.

**Sometimes you leave out words when you combine sentences.**

## Show What You Know

**Read each sentence below. Circle the two verbs and the *and* in each sentence.**

1. Barney climbs trees and eats bananas.

2. Jenny jumps on her bed and flies in the air.

3. Roland is brave and rides the fast roller coaster.

4. Sandy plays in the sand and makes sandwiches.

Score: _____     Total Possible: 12

# Practice

**Read each set of sentences. Combine them into one sentence. Circle the two verbs and the *and* that join each set.**

**1.** Samantha eats snacks all night. Samantha watches TV all night.

_____

----------------------------------------------

_____

**2.** Todd jumps for the ball. Todd catches the ball.

_____

----------------------------------------------

_____

**3.** Marsha goes to the movies. Marsha eats popcorn.

_____

----------------------------------------------

_____

# Revise

**Choose one of the sentences. Change one of the verbs. Write the new sentence.**

_____

----------------------------------------------

_____

# Tips for Your Own Writing: Revising .................

Look at a sentence you wrote for a **Practice** in another lesson. Find the subject and think how it could do more than one thing. Write the new sentence. Ask an adult to look at your work.

✎ *Sometimes a person rereads sentences and leaves out some words to turn two sentences into one.*

# 69 Grammar: Combining Sentences— Adjectives

*Words that describe paint a picture. They help you see the sentence more clearly in your mind.*

## ··············· Did You Know? ···················

**By taking a describing word from one sentence and adding it to another, you help paint a better picture of the sentence.**

I wore my tennis shoes to the picnic.
My shoes are **new.**
I wore my **new** tennis shoes to the picnic.

**A word that describes a noun is called an <u>adjective</u>.**

## Show What You Know

**Read each sentence. Circle the describing word in the second sentence. Draw an arrow to show where it fits in the first sentence.**

**Example:** We ate a watermelon and spit out the seeds.

The watermelon was juicy.

**1.** The boys and girls raced in sacks.

The sacks were burlap.

**2.** We flew kites high in the air.

The kites were plastic.

Score: _____     Total Possible: 4

# Practice

**Read each set of sentences. Circle the describing word. Write a new sentence by adding the describing word from the second sentence into the first.**

**Example:** I read a fairy tale. The fairy tale was short.
I read a **short** fairy tale.

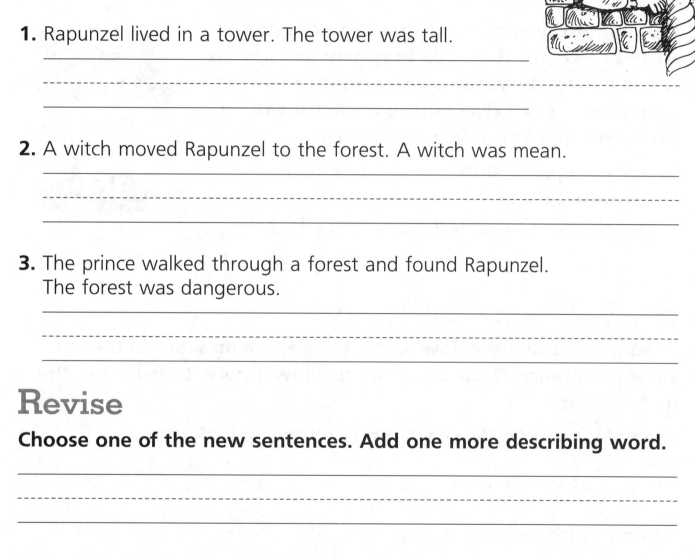

**1.** Rapunzel lived in a tower. The tower was tall.

_____

- - - - - - - - - - - - - - - - - - - - - - - - - - - -

_____

**2.** A witch moved Rapunzel to the forest. A witch was mean.

_____

- - - - - - - - - - - - - - - - - - - - - - - - - - - -

_____

**3.** The prince walked through a forest and found Rapunzel. The forest was dangerous.

_____

- - - - - - - - - - - - - - - - - - - - - - - - - - - -

_____

# Revise

**Choose one of the new sentences. Add one more describing word.**

_____

- - - - - - - - - - - - - - - - - - - - - - - - - - - -

_____

# Tips for Your Own Writing: Revising .................

Look at a story you have written. Can you find adjectives you used? Can you find a way to combine these adjectives with other sentences?

*You can write a sentence. The sentence is important. Can you combine your ideas? Then you can write an important sentence.*

**143**

# 70 Combining Sentences—Adverbs

✏️ *How do you eat—slowly, quickly, quietly, or loudly? This really can make a difference to the person sitting next to you!*

......................... **Did You Know?** ....................

**Words that describe actions or verbs are called <u>adverbs</u>. Adverbs help you see action more clearly in your mind. Sometimes you can take a word describing an action from one sentence and add it to another.**

The elephant stood on her back feet.
She stood **tall.**
The elephant stood **tall** on her back feet.

. . . . . . . . . . . . . . . . . . . . . . . . . . . . . . . . . . . . . .

## Show What You Know

**Read each sentence below. Circle the describing word in the second sentence. Draw an arrow to show where it fits best in the first sentence.**

**Example:** A monkey flipped in the air off the back of a horse.

It flipped (high).

**1.** A pretty lady spun on a rope.

She spun around.

**2.** A little clown stepped on the giant clown's toes.

He stepped hard.

Score: _____     **Total Possible: 4**

# Practice

**Read each set of sentences below. Underline the describing word in the second sentence. Then, write a new sentence by adding the describing word from the second sentence into the first sentence.**

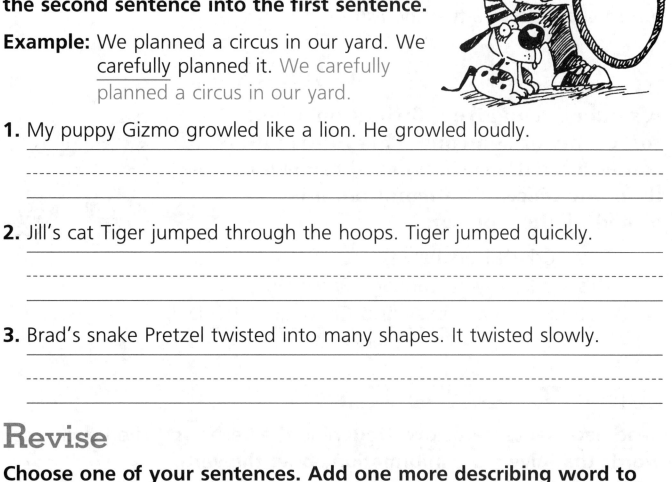

**Example:** We planned a circus in our yard. We carefully planned it. We carefully planned a circus in our yard.

**1.** My puppy Gizmo growled like a lion. He growled loudly.

_____

- - - - - - - - - - - - - - - - - - - - - - - - - -

_____

**2.** Jill's cat Tiger jumped through the hoops. Tiger jumped quickly.

_____

- - - - - - - - - - - - - - - - - - - - - - - - - -

_____

**3.** Brad's snake Pretzel twisted into many shapes. It twisted slowly.

_____

- - - - - - - - - - - - - - - - - - - - - - - - - -

_____

# Revise

**Choose one of your sentences. Add one more describing word to the action.**

_____

- - - - - - - - - - - - - - - - - - - - - - - - - -

_____

# Tips for Your Own Writing: Proofreading ..............

Look at your writing. Did you remember to add describing words to the action part of your sentence and use correct capitalization and punctuation?

*Make the words describing your actions "jump off" the paper.*

# 71 Grammar: Combining Sentences—Objects

*Go for the gold and the silver! Be like an Olympic athlete. It's fun to choose a variety of goals!*

## Did You Know?

**A sentence can give information about something or someone. This information comes after the verb. When there is more than one piece of information, it is joined by the word *and*.**

This stork delivers babies.
This stork delivers Cabbage Patch Dolls.
This stork delivers <u>babies</u> **and** <u>Cabbage Patch Dolls</u>.

## Show What You Know

**Read each sentence below. Underline the verb first. Then circle the words that give more information about the verb.**

**1.** Tooth fairies carry coins and many teeth.

**2.** Horseshoes give luck and foot support.

**3.** Genies grant wishes and desires.

**4.** A flying carpet transports magic dust and people.

**5.** A leprechaun wants gold and power.

Score: _____     **Total Possible: 15**

**146**

# Practice

**Read each set of sentences below. Combine the objects in both sentences into one smooth sentence.**

**1.** Elves make shoes. Elves make toys.

------

**2.** Magicians have magic wands. Magicians have magic hats.

------

**3.** Rabbits make colored eggs. Rabbits make chocolate bunnies.

------

**4.** Mermaids like oysters' pearls. Mermaids like sea creatures.

------

# Revise

**Choose one of your sentences. Replace one of the objects.**

------

# Tips for Your Own Writing: Proofreading ..............

Next time you write a letter, try to give a lot of information about your verbs. You can do this by adding nouns <u>after</u> the verb.

*Sometimes we need patience and hard work to make an interesting sentence.*

# 72 Review: Combining Sentences

**A.** **Combine the nouns in each set of sentences into one sentence.**

**1.** Pianos have lots of keys. Custodians have lots of keys.

-------------------------------------------------------------------

**2.** Mail carriers have many letters. Alphabets have many letters.

-------------------------------------------------------------------

**3.** Sometimes children lose their teeth. Sometimes combs lose their teeth.

-------------------------------------------------------------------

Score: _____     **Total Possible: 3**

**B.** **Combine each set of sentences into one sentence. Concentrate on the verbs.**

**1.** Big Foot wears super-sized sneakers. Big Foot takes great big steps.

-------------------------------------------------------------------

**2.** Little Bo Peep lost her sheep. Little Bo Peep bought a new leash.

-------------------------------------------------------------------

**3.** The little old woman lived in a shoe. The little old woman got the heel fixed.

-------------------------------------------------------------------

Score: _____     **Total Possible: 3**

**C. Put the describing word (adjective) from the second sentence into the first. Write the new sentence.**

**1.** Buster rode his bike on the path. His bike is muddy.

_____

_____

**2.** Goldie Goodheart loves her puppy. The puppy is playful.

_____

_____

Score: _____     Total Possible: 2

**D. Add the describing word or adverb from the second sentence into the first sentence. Write the new sentence.**

**1.** The centipede put shoes on her feet. She carefully put them on.

_____

_____

**2.** The fuzzy caterpillar changed into a butterfly. It slowly changed.

_____

_____

Score: _____     Total Possible: 2

**E. Look for the words after the verbs. Find a way to combine the sentences into a single sentence.**

**1.** Big Moose eats banana splits. Big Moose eats hamburgers.

_____

_____

**2.** Charlie Chuckles tells lots of jokes. Charlie Chuckles tells many riddles.

_____

_____

Score: _____     Total Possible: 2

REVIEW SCORE: _____     REVIEW TOTAL: 12

**149**

# Writer's Handbook
# Getting Started

 **G**et ready . . . . Get set . . . . Draw! ! !

## ⋯⋯⋯⋯⋯ Did You Know? ⋯⋯⋯⋯⋯

A picture can help you begin to write. When you add details to your picture, you get new ideas for writing.

Which picture would you choose?

Now that you have chosen your picture, step into it and look around. What do you see? List those words on paper.

Finally, write sentences about those words. As you write, you will tell your own wonderful story.

## Tips for Your Own Writing: ⋯⋯⋯⋯⋯⋯

- Create a picture that has many details.
- List words that tell about the picture.
- Write sentences using these words.

 **Y**our sentences create a picture with words!

# 2 Writer's Handbook
## Staying on the Topic

*All of the ideas in a paragraph need to be on the same track.*

## ·················· Did You Know? ··················

A paragraph is a group of sentences that tells something about the same idea. If a sentence tells about something different, remove it!

**Trisha has a toy train. It has a locomotive and eight cars. Trisha plays with many dolls. The train travels on metal tracks.**

One sentence does not belong. It does not tell about Trisha's toy train. Can you find it? It needs to be removed.

The sentence is "Trisha plays with many dolls."

Now read the paragraph. This time the sentences belong together. They all tell something about the same idea.

**Trisha has a toy train. It has a locomotive and eight cars. The train travels on metal tracks.**

## Tips for Your Own Writing: ··················

• Read your paragraph after you write it.
• Check that each sentence tells about the same idea.
• Remove sentences that do not belong.

*Learn to spot sentences that do not belong in a paragraph!*

# Writer's Handbook

## Choosing the Best Words

*Words are like apples. There are a lot to choose from, but you should always try to pick the best!*

.................... **Did You Know?** ....................

Carefully chosen words can change a simple sentence into a word picture for the reader. Read this simple sentence:

**She made a pie.**

Is the sentence the best it can be? Let's change a word.

**She baked a pie.**

Now we know that the pie was cooked. Let's make another change.

**Mrs. MacDonald baked a pie.**

Now we know who did the baking. Let's make one more change.

**Mrs. MacDonald baked an apple pie.**

With a few simple changes we changed the sentence into a word picture for the reader.

## Tips for Your Own Writing: ....................

• Think of new words that would make your writing better. (See *Word List* on page 160.)
• See whether there are other ways to make your sentences more interesting and easier to understand.

*Be a good writer and choose your words carefully!*

# Writer's Handbook
# Correcting Mistakes

*O*ops! We all make mistakes, but that's why we cross out and make changes—to make our writing better.

## ·················· Did You Know? ··················

A good writer is also a detective. A good writer examines each sentence. When something isn't exactly right, a good writer makes a note and decides what to do next.

The paragraph below has thirteen mistakes.

**the cookee jar wuz empty. what happened two the last cookee mi little brother's hands wer clean. The  mystery wuz solved when i saw Dad he gave me a kiss, and I smelled cookies!**

Now here is the same story after the mistakes were corrected.

**The cookie jar was empty. What happened to the last cookie? My little brother's hands were clean. The mystery was solved when I saw Dad. He gave me a kiss, and I smelled cookies!**

## Tips for Your Own Writing: ·······················

- ✔ Check that words are spelled correctly.
- ◯◯ See if all sentences begin with capital letters.
- 🛑 Stop! Choose the correct ending mark for each sentence.

*B*ecome a writing detective! Find your mistakes and correct them.

# Writer's Handbook
# Telling a Story

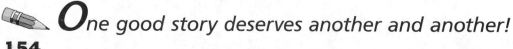 *The child said to his parents, "I want to hear a story."*
*They said to him, "You tell us a story."*

## ..................... Did You Know? .....................

When you narrate, you tell a story. Your characters are involved in what happens in the story. Some characters may have to solve a problem. Your story needs a **beginning,** a **middle,** and an **end.**

**A little dragon asked the king if he could work in the castle. The king thought about what the dragon could do. In the winter, he could warm the castle with his hot breath. In the summer, the dragon could cool the castle by wagging his long tail. The dragon liked the idea. He is still working in the castle today.**

Who were the characters in the story? What was the problem? What was the story's beginning, middle, and end?

## Tips for Your Own Writing: .........................

- Think of a problem.
- Plan a beginning, a middle, and an end.
- Read your story to see if it is easy to understand.
- Make any needed changes and corrections.

*One good story deserves another and another!*

# Writer's Handbook
# Writing to Convince

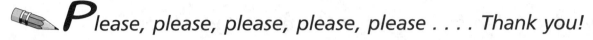 *P*lease, please, please, please, please . . . . Thank you!

## ...................... Did You Know? ......................

Sometimes we write to make others accept our way of thinking. Using important facts or ideas that are true helps convince others.

Which paragraph will convince parents to allow children to watch more TV?

**Children deserve to watch more TV. Kids need to relax. Sometimes they get bored. Watching TV is fun for them.**

or

**Children learn by watching TV. They see people and animals from around the world. They watch the news and learn about sports. Watching nature programs even helps students do better in school.**

Parents would probably be more convinced after reading the second paragraph. Information that fits with their wishes makes it more likely for them to see the benefits of watching television.

## Tips for Your Own Writing: ...........................

• Use true facts and appropriate information to help convince others.
• Check to see whether your sentences are clear and easy to understand.
• Read your paragraph and make improvements.

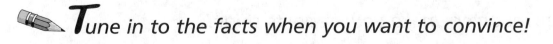 *T*une in to the facts when you want to convince!

# Writer's Handbook
## Writing a Report

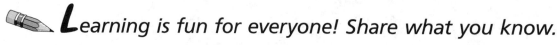 *Learning is fun for everyone! Share what you know.*

### ················· Did You Know? ·················

We learn by sharing ideas. Reports help you share what you know. To write a good report, use the following tips from this star reporter:

1. Choose a topic that interests you. If you're not interested, your readers won't be either.

2. Read books and magazines that have information about your topic. Pictures also help you learn.

3. List the important facts.

4. Write your report. Keep on the topic!

5. Read your report and make any needed changes and corrections.

The following paragraph is an example of a good report:

> **Some animals have interesting eating habits. Raccoons wet their food before they eat it. Elephants sometimes eat 23 hours each day. An anteater may eat 30,000 ants in one day. Camels can drink more than 12 gallons of water in 10 minutes. Wouldn't it be fun to invite them all for dinner?**

## Tips for Your Own Writing: ···················

- Choose interesting ideas and avoid boring topics.
- Read as much information about your topic as you can.
- Read your report and check for any mistakes.

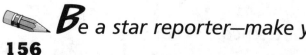 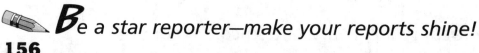 *Be a star reporter—make your reports shine!*

# Writer's Handbook

## 8 Writing a Friendly Letter

*Signed . . . sealed . . . and delivered! Sending and getting mail is fun!*

### ..................... Did You Know? ...................

In a friendly letter, you can share news. You can ask questions. You can even show someone that you care about them.

---

July 5, 2000

Dear Oobie,

I was so glad to see you yesterday. I'm sorry that you had to leave so soon. Did you have a nice trip home? Did you see any fireworks as you zoomed through space? We had the biggest fireworks display ever in our town after you left. I'll bet that your planet is really cool. Maybe I can visit you next year.

Your friend,

Jimmy Lee

P.S. You are really "out-of-this-world"!

---

## Tips for Your Own Writing: .........................

- Decide on someone who would like to hear from you.
- Share some news.
- Ask questions.
- Show that you care.
- Read and check your letter. Did you sign your name?

*Letters bring smiles across the miles!*

# Writer's Handbook
# Writing a Poem

*N*o time to rhyme? Here is a poem for you!

## ...................... Did You Know? ......................

A diamante poem is shaped a little like a diamond. Every line tells about one topic. The lines do not need to rhyme. Here is one form:

*First line:* one noun, or word, that names a thing

*Second line:* two adjectives, or words, that describe that thing

*Third line:* three verbs with *-ing* endings

*Fourth line:* two adjectives

*Fifth line:* one noun

**Puppy**

**Little, furry**

**Wagging, playing, barking**

**Frisky, friendly**

**Gizmo**

## Tips for Your Own Writing: ...........................

- Choose an object or creature that really interests you.
- Select adjectives and verbs that tell about your object or creature.
- Read your poem. Are there better words to use? (See *Word List* on page 160.)
- Exchange a word for a new word and listen to your new poem. Which version is best?

*P*olish your poems with words that sparkle!

# 10 Writer's Handbook
## Writing Directions

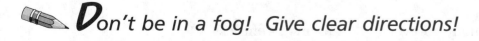 *Unclear directions are like coming to a fork in the road. Where do you go next?*

### ...................... Did You Know? ......................

Directions tell how to do something. They need to be very clear. Compare the two sets of directions below.

**Walk down the path for a while until you see the path divide. Look under the bush.**

or

**You can find my pot of gold. First, begin at the "x" made with sticks on the path. Then walk exactly 250 feet until you come to where the path divides. Next, go left 10 feet. Finally, stop at the golden-colored bush. Look underneath.**

The second directions are much better. They explain where you are going. Then they clearly tell how to get there.

## Tips for Your Own Writing: ..........................

• Tell what the other persons will find if they follow your directions.
• Write all the steps in the correct order.
• Use words like *first, next, then,* and *finally* to help tell the order.

*Don't be in a fog! Give clear directions!*

# Writer's Handbook
# Synonym Word List

Good . . . Better . . . Best! ! !

The **bold** words on the left are often used in stories. They are not always the best choice. Try replacing them with some of the other word choices given and see if your writing improves. Choose words that best help your writing!

## NOUNS:

**baby**—child, infant, toddler
**dad**—father, daddy, pop
**dog**—mutt, puppy
**friend**—chum, pal, partner, buddy
**gift**—present

**love**—affection, kindness, devotion
**mistake**—error, blunder
**mom**—mother, mommy
**price**—cost, tab, charge
**road**—highway, lane, street, avenue

## VERBS:

**ask**—beg, demand, plead, question
**begin**—start, commence
**bite**—chew, chomp, nibble, munch
**break**—crack, collapse, crumple, crash
**bring**—fetch, get, carry
**come**—arrive, enter, reach
**cry**—bawl, sob, shout
**do**—complete, finish
**drink**—swallow, sip, gulp
**eat**—devour, gobble
**end**—complete, finish
**find**—discover, locate
**get**—collect, gain, gather, win

**give**—grant, present
**go**—move, travel
**have**—own, possess, keep
**hug**—embrace, squeeze, hold
**know**—recognize, understand
**laugh**—chuckle, giggle, snicker
**pull**—tug, drag
**put**—place, lay
**run**—race, scurry, dash, scamper
**see**—notice, observe
**smile**—grin
**surprise**—amaze, startle
**tell**—announce, mention, report

## ADJECTIVES:

**bad**—cruel, horrible, mean, nasty, terrible
**big**—enormous, great, huge, large, wide
**brave**—bold, confident, fearless
**bright**—gleaming, shiny, sparkling
**dark**—black, gloomy, shadowy
**easy**—simple, moderate
**funny**—clownish, foolish, silly
**good**—delicious, yummy
**great**—important, wonderful
**happy**—cheerful, joyful
**last**— final, closing
**little**—small, tiny

**loud**—noisy
**nice**—loving, pleasant, tender
**old**—ancient, aged
**pretty**—beautiful, lovely, gorgeous
**quiet**—calm, silent, still
**rich**—wealthy, affluent, sweet
**sad**—gloomy, unhappy
**shy**—bashful, timid
**smart**—clever, sharp
**thin**—lean, narrow, slim, slender
**ugly**—frightful, horrible, hideous

## ADVERBS:

**always**—constantly, continually, forever
**early**—shortly, soon
**fast**—quickly, speedily

**forever**—endless
**often**—frequently
**really**—truly

**160**

# SPECTRUM

# Language Arts

## Grade 2
## Answer Key

# Lesson 1

## Lesson 1  Capitalization: First Word in a Sentence

Use a capital letter to begin each sentence. The capital is like a green traffic light. **Go!**

........................... **Did You Know?** ...........

The capital letter at the beginning of each sentence often tells you that it is time to take a breath. Whew!

**S**ome snakes act like a baby's toy. **T**hey like to rattle.

### Show What You Know

Circle each word below that should begin with a capital letter.

(a) little snake could not see very well. (he) tried to wrap himself

around a tree. (the) tree began to walk. (it) was really an elephant's leg.

(then) the snake fell in love. (his) girlfriend turned out to be a garden hose.

(now) the snake wears glasses.

Score: _____    Total Possible: 7

6

### Proofread

Read this story about an unlucky snake. Circle three letters that need to be capitalized. Write the capital letter above each one.

**Example:** (W)e go to (A)unt Ann's house every (T)hanksgiving.

The little snake did not feel well. (F)irst, he bit his lip. (T)hen, he had a

frog in his throat. Finally, he took some aspirin. (N)ow he is much better.

### Practice

Write two sentences about the picture. Do not forget to use capital letters.

1. _____
   Review the sentences to be sure your child has:
   • capitalized the first word of each sentence.
   • written clear sentences.

2. _____
   _____
   _____

### Tips for Your Own Writing: Proofreading ...........

Look at a story you have written. Are you ready to **Go** at the beginning of each sentence? Did you begin each sentence with a capital letter?

**B**egin each sentence in a big way—with a capital letter.

7

...........................................................................

# Lesson 2

## Lesson 2  Capitalization: The Word *I*

**T**he word I is always a capital letter.

........................ **Did You Know?** .........

You are a very important person. When you use *I* in place of your name, make it a capital letter.

**I** love sports!
My dad and **I** play catch together.
So far the only thing **I** have caught is a cold!

### Show What You Know

Read this poem. Circle each word *i* that should be a capital letter.

My dad and (I) went fishing.

We went to Rainbow Lake.

(I) thought (I)'d catch a fish.

It would be a piece of cake.

(I) sat and sat for hours.

The fish just would not bite.

(I) finally told the worms,

"I'm going home. Good night."

Score: _____    Total Possible: 5

8

### Proofread

Read each sentence below. Circle six letters that need to be capitals. Write the capital letter above each one.

I am an insect, and (I) can do what I am. What am (I)? (I) am a fly!

(I) am round on the ends and high in the middle. What am (I)? (I) am Ohio!

### Practice

Pretend that you are a football or soccer player. Write two sentences about what you would be doing. Do not forget to use capital letters!

1. _____
   Review the sentences to be sure your child has:
   • capitalized the word *I*.
   • written sentences that make sense.

2. _____
   _____
   _____

### Tips for Your Own Writing: Proofreading ...........

Read something you have written about yourself. Did you use a capital *I* when you talked about yourself?

**C**apital letters can be eye (I)—catching!

9

# Lesson 3

### Lesson 3 Capitalization: People and Pets

*Your name makes you very special. People notice names because they begin with capital letters.*

...................... **Did You Know?** ......................

A person's name or a pet's name always begins with a capital letter.

**M**ike and his dog **S**kimpy used an air pump at the gas station.

**M**ike's dad told **M**ike to pump up **S**kimpy's air mattress.

## Show What You Know

**Circle each word below that should begin with a capital letter.**

The owners and their pets were ready to make the new movie.

(allison) walked her pet alligator (choppers) through the car wash to clean

his teeth. (gordon) and his pet gorilla (harry) climbed the jungle gym. (libby)

and her lion (kitty) took lots of catnaps. The movie starred my elephant

(ellie) and was a huge success!

Score: _____   Total Possible: 7

10

---

## Proofread

**Read the poem below. Circle seven letters that need to be capitalized. Then write the capital letter above each one.**

Sam has a snake named (s)linky.

It slides across the floor.

(i)t goes for (r)ex, a lizard,

but (r)ex runs out the door.

(j)ack owns a dog named Arf.

He loves a cat called Mew.

When (a)rf and (m)ew eat lunch,

they always chat and chew.

## Practice

**Write two sentences about people and their pets. Be sure to name each person and pet.**

1. Review the sentences to be sure your child has:
   • capitalized the names of people and pets.
   • written sentences that make sense.

2. _____

### Tips for Your Own Writing: Proofreading ..............

Look at your own writing. Read something you have written about someone you know. Have you used a capital letter to begin every name?

*Use capital letters for names.*

11

---

# Lesson 4

### Lesson 4 Capitalization: Titles of Relatives

*Royal families are not the only ones to have titles. People in **everyone's** family have titles. You are as special as a prince or a princess!*

...................... **Did You Know?** ......................

A person's name always begins with a capital letter. When a title is added before a name, the title usually begins with a capital letter, too.

**U**ncle **F**arley **F**arkle and **A**unt **F**ranny **F**arkle fed peanuts to their cows. **U**ncle **F**arley and **A**unt **F**ranny hoped to get peanut butter instead of milk! The **F**arkles tend to be a little silly.

## Show What You Know

**Circle each word below that should begin with a capital letter.**

(uncle) Farley and (aunt) Franny invited their family to stay at the farm. First, (cousin) Fifi Farkle and (cousin) Freddy Farkle came in their "pig-up" truck. At midnight, (grandpa) Fletcher Farkle and (grandma) Frieda Farkle finally arrived. (grandpa) Farkle had stopped to buy a hammer so that he could hit the hay when he arrived.

Score: _____   Total Possible: 7

12

---

## Proofread

**Read the story below. Circle four words that need to begin with a capital letter. Then write the capital letter above each one.**

Everyone had fun on the Farkle farm. (c)ousin Fifi helped Grandma

Farkle plant eggs to grow eggplants. (c)ousin Freddy and (g)randpa Farkle

tried to play horseshoes with (a)unt Franny, but they could not get the

shoes off the horse.

## Practice

**Write two sentences about the Farkle relatives. Give each person a title and a name.**

1. Review the sentences to be sure your child has:
   • capitalized each relative's title.
   • applied earlier lessons on capitals.
   • written sentences that make sense.

2. _____

### Tips for Your Own Writing: Proofreading ..............

Next time you write to someone in your family, check your titles. Did you remember that titles are capitalized when placed before names?

*Show your relatives that you think they are important. Use capital letters!*

13

# Lesson 5

### Lesson 5 Capitalization: Titles of Respect

*BIG people's titles begin with BIG letters to show respect.*

....................... **Did You Know?** .......................

**Miss, Mrs., Ms., and Mr.** are titles of respect and should be used before adult names. Begin each title with a capital letter.

**M**r. and **M**rs. Rodeo
had a son named Buck.
He became a famous rider.
He was known as **M**r. Buck.

### Show What You Know

**Circle each word below that should begin with a capital letter.**

(mrs.) Trotter rode her horse.

It bucked her in the air.

(mr.) Trotter caught his wife.

This gave her quite a scare!

(mr.) Trotter took his wife

And showed her how to ride.

He found a gentle horse for her.

Now (mrs.) Trotter rides with pride!

Score: _____   Total Possible: 4

14

### Proofread

**Read the poem below. Circle four letters that need to be capitalized. Write the capital letter above each one.**

Little (m)iss Short likes to twirl — *M*

A rope around the cows.

Big (m)r. Stretch rides to win — *M*

And likes to take big bows.

(m)r. Steer and Mrs. Steer — *M*

Once tried to tame a bull.

(m)rs. Calf arrived to help, — *M*

But the bull had too much pull!

### Practice

**Write two sentences about these people: Miss Brand, Mrs. Chaps, Ms. Spurs, and Mr. Buckaroo.**

1. Review the sentences to be sure your child has:
   • capitalized each person's title of respect.
   • applied earlier lessons on capitals.
   • written sentences that make sense.

2. _____

### Tips for Your Own Writing: Proofreading ..............

Next time you write a letter to an adult, be sure to show respect. Use capital letters for the title.

*Show respect for adults in a **big** way! Use capital letters when you call them Miss, Mrs., Ms., or Mr.*

15

........................................................................

# Lesson 6

### Lesson 6 Review: Capitalization

**A. Read the paragraph below. Circle eleven letters that should be capitalized. Write the capital letter above each one.**

My little sister (a)nnie and (i) have a lot of fun together. (w)e go to the park almost every day in the summer. (i) like to swing. Annie likes to climb on the monkey bars. When (u)ncle (l)ee and (a)unt Susie come to visit, they go to the park with us. (w)e usually pack a picnic lunch to take along. (t)hey have as much fun as (a)nnie and (i).

Score: _____   Total Possible: 11

**B. Read the sentences below. Circle ten letters that need to be capitalized. Write the capital letter above each one.**

1. (m)other (g)oose took flying lessons from an eagle pilot.

2. (l)ittle (m)iss (m)uffet went to the store to buy bug spray.

3. (m)r. and (m)rs. (s)prat loved to eat fast food.

4. (m)ary and (i) took her lamb home from school.

Score: _____   Total Possible: 10

16

**C. Read the sentences below. Write the correct capital letter in each blank. You will use an I, M, or G for each blank.**

I just invented a magic pencil. __M__ y magic pencil did all my
1

math homework for __M__ rs. Benson. __I__ could not believe that all
2                          3

the math was correct! __I__ wrote a letter to __M__ r. and
4                              5

__M__ rs. Lee in Chinese. __I__ don't even know Chinese! When my
6                        7

magic pencil broke its lead, it grew new lead. __I__ wrote the
8

President a letter. The President invited me to visit him at the White

House. __I__ showed my pencil to __G__ randpa Wise. __G__ randpa
9                        10                          11

Wise told me that the magic really comes from my heart and my head.

Score: _____   Total Possible: 11

REVIEW SCORE: _____   REVIEW TOTAL: 32

17

**164**   Answer Key

# Lesson 7

## Lesson 7 Capitalization: Places

✎ *Your writing will not go far if you do not place a capital letter at the beginning of names of places.*

### .................... Did You Know? ....................

**There are many kinds of places. Use a capital letter for the first letter of the name of each special place.**

Sue visited the **K**alamazoo **Z**oo. (zoo)
Dinah is from **N**orth **C**arolina. (state)
Gail stayed overnight in **V**ail. (city)
Pete lives on **S**weet **S**treet. (street)
Jewel goes to **L**iverpool **S**chool. (school)
Erica was born in the **U**nited **S**tates of **A**merica. (country)

### Show What You Know

**Circle each word below that should begin with a capital.**

In (america) there really is a city called (baker). It is in the state of (oregon). Do the children in (baker) attend (chocolate) (cake) (school) on (frosting) (street)? We would have to visit (oregon) to find the answer.

Score: _____ Total Possible: 10

18

## Proofread

**Read this report about Disney World. Circle ten words that need to be capitalized. Write the capital letter above each one.**

Many people visit (disney) World in (orlando), (florida). A lot of these
people come from the United (states) of (america). You can visit (disney)
(world) in other places in the world, too. Mickey Mouse and his friends are
in (tokyo), (japan), and Paris, (france).

## Practice

**Write a sentence that tells the city and state where you live. Write another sentence that tells the name of your school.**

1. Review the sentences to be sure your child has:
   • capitalized the name of each place.
   • written sentences that make sense.

2. _____

## Tips for Your Own Writing: Proofreading ..............

Next time you write about a special place, be sure to use a capital letter to begin the names of countries, states, cities, and streets.

✎ *Begin each trip to a special place with a capital letter.*

19

---

# Lesson 8

## Lesson 8 Capitalization: Days and Months

✎ *Mark your calendar with capitals! Begin days of the week and months of the year with capital letters.*

### .................... Did You Know? ....................

**There are seven days in the week and twelve months in a year. Those nineteen words always begin with a capital letter.**

**S**unday, **M**onday, **T**uesday, **W**ednesday, **T**hursday, **F**riday, **S**aturday

**J**anuary, **F**ebruary, **M**arch, **A**pril, **M**ay, **J**une, **J**uly, **A**ugust, **S**eptember, **O**ctober, **N**ovember, **D**ecember

### Show What You Know

**Read this poem. Circle each letter that should be capitalized.**

On (m)onday Millie made a cake.

She slept all day and it did bake.

On Tuesday Tony saw the smoke

And shook his sister till she woke.

That was (a)pril of last year

Or so I heard from sister dear.

If Millie made a pie in (j)une

Will it not be ready soon?

Score: _____ Total Possible: 3

20

## Proofread

**Read each riddle below. Circle each letter that needs to be capitalized. Write the capital letter above it. There are three mistakes.**

1. Why is (s)unday the smartest day of the week? **It is the brightest.**

2. Why do soldiers dislike (m)arch? **It hurts their feet.**

3. When is (m)ay a polite month? **When it is used with the words "I please."**

## Practice

**Write one sentence about the day of the week you like best. Write another sentence to tell which month you like best.**

1. Review the sentences to be sure your child has:
   • capitalized days of the week and months of the year.
   • written sentences that make sense.

2. _____

## Tips for Your Own Writing: Proofreading ..............

Reread a journal entry. Did you begin your day of the week and month of the year with capital letters?

✎ *Start each day of the week and each month of the year with a smile . . . and a capital letter!*

21

## Lesson 9 Capitalization: Friendly Letters

*Friendly letters are letters you write to friends. Use capital letters for important parts of friendly letters.*

...................... **Did You Know?** ......................

Friendly letters begin with the date at the top. Always use a capital letter for the name of the month—**A**ugust 10, 2000.

**Start** your greeting with *Dear*. **Then** write your friend's name. Begin each word with a capital—Dear **P**atrick,

The body of the letter is what you want to tell your friend. Use capital letters to begin each sentence.

You end the letter with a closing and your name. Use a capital letter to begin the closing. Begin your name with a capital letter, too—**S**incerely,
     **C**indy

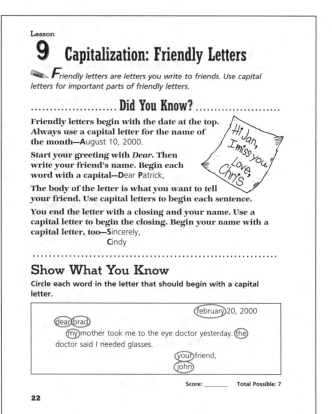

Hi Jan,
I miss you.
Love,
Chris

### Show What You Know

Circle each word in the letter that should begin with a capital letter.

february 20, 2000

dear brad,
    my mother took me to the eye doctor yesterday. the doctor said I needed glasses.
            your friend,
            john

Score: _____    Total Possible: 7

22

### Proofread

Read the letter below. Circle seven letters that should be capitalized. Write the capital letter above each one.

                                        N
                            november 10, 2000

    D   J
    dear jimmy,
        I                 E          I
        work like a horse. eat like a bird. am as tired as a
    dog. Everyone tells me to see a vet.

            Sincerely,
                S
            Sam smith

### Practice

Think of a relative. Write a greeting and the first sentence of a friendly letter to that relative.

Review the writing to be sure your child has:
1.  • followed the form of a greeting
    • written a sentence that makes sense
2.  • capitalized the greeting and the beginning word of the sentence.

### Tips for Your Own Writing: Proofreading ...........

The next time you write a letter, look at the important parts. Did you use capitals for them?

*Make your letters "letter-perfect." Capitals show what is important!*

23

## Lesson 10 Review: Capitalization

**A.** Read Samantha's letter below. Circle 21 letters that should be capitalized. Write the capital letter above each one.

                                J
                            july 29, 2000
    D
    dear Mom and Dad,
        T        T        C
        today is tuesday. camp Swampy is really neat. All the
                          I            F      H
    bugs are very big. have a spider named fuzzy. her legs
                  I              M        S
    have a lot of hair. put her in a jar on monday. spike is my
            H                          K
    snake. he sleeps with me in my sleeping bag. kyle, the
                                  S      I
    adult who stays in my tent, doesn't know about spike.
        S        F
    will show you spike and fuzzy when I come home in
    A      I
    august. cannot wait to see what I will find tomorrow!
            L
            love,
            S
            samantha

Score: _____    Total Possible: 21

24

**B.** Read Joshua's letter below. Circle each letter that should be capitalized. Write the capital letter above each one. There are 22 letters to capitalize.

                                J
                            june 16, 2000
    D
    dear Grandma and Grandpa,
        I            I    D          S
        miss you so much! do you think spot will remember
            I                              I
    me? know that you will think I have grown taller. hope
        T              O   A
    that tommy, my friend on oak avenue, will still be my
            I              I
    friend. hope my bike is not rusty. started this letter two
            M                    O   F
    days ago. mom says that I should mail it today. on friday
            M   R        S   D      W
    we are going to mount rushmore in south dakota. we will
    meet some really big presidents. See you later!
            L
            love,
            J
            joshua

Score: _____    Total Possible: 22

REVIEW SCORE: _____    REVIEW TOTAL: 43

25

# Lesson 11

### Lesson
# 11 Punctuation: Periods

✎ *Use a period to end a sentence that tells something. It is like a stop sign.* **Stop.**

...................... **Did You Know?** ...................

**A period at the end of a sentence shows you that a statement is finished.**

Cows like to dance so that they can make milk shakes**.**

Chickens like to spin around so that they can make scrambled eggs**.**

## Show What You Know

**Put a slash (/) at the end of each sentence.**

Animals and people might have funny favorite foods/An elephant

may like squash/Some fish may choose watermelon/Sheep may be very

happy to get baa-nanas/Goats eat canned anything/Scared people may

eat chicken/My favorite food is hay because I eat like a horse/

Score: _____  Total Possible: 7

26

## Proofread

**Read the story below. Five periods are missing. Circle the words that should have periods after them.**

Oscar was very (hungry)He decided to make a big sandwich. First, he

got a huge loaf of (bread)Then, he added some ham and cheese. Next,

he put on some (pickles)Oscar added bananas, strawberries, and whipped

cream. Oscar took a (bite)His sandwich did not taste very (good)

## Practice

**Write two sentences that tell something about a game you like. End each sentence with a period.**

1. Review the sentences to be sure your child has:
   • placed a period at the end of each sentence.
   • written sentences that make sense.

2. _____

## Tips for Your Own Writing: Proofreading

Look at something you have written. Did you use a period to end each telling sentence?

✎ *Don't forget to* **stop** *at the end of a telling sentence with a period.*

27

··········································································································

# Lesson 12

### Lesson
# 12 Punctuation: Question Marks

✎ *Use a question mark to end a sentence that asks something.*

...................... **Did You Know?** ....................

**Sentences that ask questions end with a question mark.**

Why did the cow jump over the moon?
He wanted to get to the Milky Way.

## Show What You Know

**Read the story below. There should be a question mark after each asking sentence. Circle each word that should have a question mark after it.**

Starry Knight was an astronaut. She was ready to fly into space.

Where did she put her (food)It was in her launch box. Did she forget

(anything)Starry brought a mop to clean up any stardust. What was

(missing)Starry ran to get a shovel. She might need to dig a black hole.

Would the trip be (interesting)Ms. Knight would soon find out.

Score: _____  Total Possible: 4

28

## Proofread

**Read the story below. Circle three words that should have question marks after them.**

Starry Knight's rocket blasted off. She landed on a new planet.

Would she meet strange (creatures)Would they be (friendly)Starry climbed

out of the rocket. She saw a purple, three-headed creature. What was it?

Was it (friendly)It told her that it liked to eat vegetables. It asked if she

were a vegetable. Starry Knight left quickly.

## Practice

**Write two asking sentences about outer space. Put a question mark at the end of each sentence.**

1. Review the sentences to be sure your child has:
   • placed a question mark at the end of each asking sentence.
   • written sentences that make sense.

2. _____

## Tips for Your Own Writing: Proofreading

Check some of your writing to find asking sentences. Did you end each one with a question mark?

✎ *Question marks ask questions like teachers do. Who knows the answers?*

29

# Lesson 13

### Lesson
## 13 Punctuation: Periods and Question Marks

✎ *Stop at the end of each sentence. If the sentence tells something, use a period. If the sentence asks something, use a question mark.*

............ **Did You Know?** .......

**Telling sentences always end with a period. Asking sentences always end with a question mark.**

Why is the dinosaur stopping?
He came to the end of the road.

## Show What You Know
**Underline each telling sentence. Circle each asking sentence.**

Mother Dinosaur was cleaning house She wanted Father Dinosaur to help move some of the large rocks around the cave How would he do this What would be the easiest way to help Mother Dinosaur Father Dinosaur thought and thought What should he do Finally, he decided to eat lots of spinach Then he could use his own dino-mite

Score: _____ Total Possible: 8

30

## Proofread
**Most riddles begin with an asking sentence and end with a telling sentence. Read each dinosaur riddle. Write a 1 before the asking part of the riddle and add a question mark at the end where it is needed. Write a 2 before the telling part of the riddle and add a period at the end where it is needed.**

__1__ / 1  What is a stegosaurus's favorite sport?

__2__ / 2  Volleyball, because she can spike the ball.

__2__ / 3  She stood too close to the pencil sharpener.

__1__ / 4  How did the triceratops get pointy horns?

## Practice
**Write one question and one statement about dinosaurs.**

1. Review the sentences to be sure your child has:
   • used periods and question marks correctly.
   • written sentences that make sense.

2. _____

## Tips for Your Own Writing: Proofreading ..........
Read a piece of your writing. Did you put a period after each telling sentence and a question mark after each asking sentence?

✎ *Sentences, like stories, need correct endings. Otherwise they do not make sense.*

31

---

# Lesson 14

### Lesson
## 14 Punctuation: Exclamation Points

✎ *Wow! It is exciting to use an exclamation point!*

.............. **Did You Know?** ...............

**Sentences that show surprise or excitement end with an exclamation point. Read exclamatory sentences louder than others and use lots of expression!**

Look out! Something with four eyes and sixteen legs is climbing up the house!

## Show What You Know
**Read each set of sentences. Circle each sentence that shows excitement and should end with an exclamation point.**

King Kong just stepped on our piano and the keys went flat.

We play the piano at home.

Mom is washing our clothes.

Something is moving in the laundry basket.

A foot has twelve inches.

Big Foot is hiding behind that tree.

Score: _____ Total Possible: 3

32

## Proofread
**Read the poem below. Add one period and two exclamation points where they are needed.**

My friend and I went swimming.

We swam a long, long while.

We floated and we splashed about.

And then we saw a crocodile!

The croc swam 'round in circles.

We were sad to leave so soon.

It was 11:55.

And crocodiles eat at noon!

## Practice
**Write two exciting sentences about something you have done. Be sure to end each sentence with an exclamation point.**

1. Review the sentences to be sure your child has:
   • used exclamation points correctly.
   • written sentences that make sense.

2. _____

## Tips for Your Own Writing: Proofreading ..........
Read aloud with expression a story you have written. Did you use exclamation points for your exciting sentences?

✎ *Exclamation points are like periods that explode with excitement!*

33

# Lesson 15

**A. Read the poem below about cats. Add seven missing periods, three question marks, and two exclamation points.**

Tom the tomcat moved to town.

He was acting tough!

What did others think of Tom?

He was mean and rough!

Wise the dog soon heard of Tom.

He could make things right.

The dog would talk to Tom.

Would Tom really want to fight?

Tom listened to the dog.

Wise was really smart.

Did Tom learn he should be kind?

Yes, he had a change of heart.

Score: _____   Total Possible: 12

34

**B. Read the sentences below about clowns. Add four missing periods, two question marks, and two exclamation points.**

Willy, Billy, and Lily are circus clowns.

Who is the silliest clown?

Willy has a squirting flower.

Oh no, he squirted me in the eye!

Billy has big, big shoes.

Billy just stepped on my foot!

When Lily sings, her ears wiggle.

Who is the silliest clown?

Score: _____   Total Possible: 8

**C. Read the following sentences. Mixed-up Martha ended four sentences with the wrong marks. Circle each wrong mark and write the correct one at the end.**

Greta Green grew grapes(!).          Wanda and Wendy wondered(?).

Her friend Fried F. Frost fished(?).   Super Sally said she knew.

Both bought books about boats.         Do you?

Why(.)?

Score: _____   Total Possible: 8

REVIEW SCORE: _____   REVIEW TOTAL: 28

35

# Lesson 16

✎ *Commas are sometimes used between words in sentences. They tell the reader to pause for a very short time before finishing the sentence.*

..................... **Did You Know?** .....................

**A comma goes between the day and the year.**

How old will you be on January 1, 2100

**A comma goes between the name of a city and state. A comma also goes after the state if it is in the middle of a sentence.**

A train just left the station in Boston, Massachusetts, with the President on board.

## Show What You Know

**Read this paragraph. Put a slash (/) between each day and year. Also put a slash between the names of cities and states.**

The train arrived in Albany/New York, on March 13/2000. It

continued down the track until it reached Philadelphia/Pennsylvania. It

was sidetracked there until March 15/2000. The train finally arrived in

Baltimore/Maryland, on March 19/2000. From there, the train brought

the President home to the White House.

Score: _____   Total Possible: 6

36

## Proofread

**Add five commas where they are needed.**

My class was studying about unusual names of cities in the United

States. I began my report on February 6, 2000. I read about Boulder,

Colorado. I wonder if the rocks in that city are bigger than the rocks in

Little Rock, Arkansas. Do ghosts really live in Casper, Wyoming? Does

everyone sew in Needles, California? I finished my report on February 12,

2000. By the way, I live in Reading, Pennsylvania.

## Practice

**Write a sentence that tells your birth date. Then write another sentence that names your city and state.**

1. _Review the sentences to be sure_
   _your child has:_
   _• used commas correctly._
   _• written sentences that make sense._

2. _____

## Tips for Your Own Writing: Proofreading ............

Look at a report you have written. Did you put a comma between the day and year, and also between the city and state?

✎ *Commas make reading easier to understand. Pause when you see a comma!*

37

Answer Key **169**

# Lesson 17

### Lesson
# 17 Punctuation: Commas in Friendly Letters

*Commas are used in friendly letters. They tell the reader to pause.*

#### ................ Did You Know? ................

**Put a comma between the day and year in the date—**January 4, 2000

**Put a comma after a greeting.**
Dear Cinderella,

**Put a comma after a closing.**
Love,
Prince Charming

## Show What You Know

**Read this letter. Put a slash (/) where commas are needed.**

> September 17/1598
>
> Dear Rapunzel/
>
> I have heard that you have the longest hair in the kingdom. Why do you let the prince climb up your hair? Shouldn't he get the elevator fixed?
>
> Your friend/
> Sleeping Beauty

Score: _____  Total Possible: 3

38

## Proofread

**Add two commas where they are needed.**

> September 25,1598
>
> Dear Sleeping Beauty,
> The prince climbed my hair only once. He had to go chase a dragon. He had stopped at the market first to buy a fire alarm. (We finally got the elevator fixed!)
> Sincerely,
> Rapunzel

## Practice

**Write a date, a greeting, and a closing for a letter. Don't forget the commas!**
Sample answers are given.

Date: _March 15, 2000_

Greeting: _Dear Cinderella,_

Closing: _Love,_

Writer's Name: _The prince_ Review the letters to be sure your child has added commas where they belong.

## Tips for Your Own Writing: Proofreading ..............

Next time you write a friendly letter, read it aloud. Did you pause a little after the commas in the date, the greeting, and the closing?

*Commas in letter parts show readers where to slow down and take a quick breath. Commas are for pausing.*

39

. . . . . . . . . . . . . . . . . . . . . . . . . . . . . . . . . . . . . . . . . . . . .

# Lesson 18

### Lesson
# 18 Punctuation: Commas in Lists

*Commas are used in lists of three or more. They let you know there are more than two items that belong together.*

#### ................ Did You Know? ........

**A comma goes between each person, place, thing, or phrase in a list.**

Did you hear about the Big Mac-Intosh computer? It comes with a bun, burger, cheese, lettuce, and special sauce!

## Show What You Know

**The story below is confusing. Help the story make sense by putting a slash (/) to show where commas are needed between the words or phrases in the lists.**

Dad sent me to the store to buy a melon/a cucumber/some olives/ and some sugar. When I got to the store, I could not remember what I was supposed to get. I knew something was round/something was long/ something could fit on my fingers/and something was sweet. So I bought a ball/a bat/a ring/and some candy.

Score: _____  Total Possible: 9

40

## Proofread

**Read each sentence below. Make the lists in the sentences easier to read by putting seven commas where they are needed.**

1. Fleas, flies, bees, and beetles drive Bertha buggy.

2. What is slimy, slippery, sloppy, sluggish, and silver? I do not know, but it is sitting on top of your head!

3. Mrs. Bryant sometimes confuses the names of her quadruplets Bruce, Brice, Brian, and Bruno.

## Practice

**Make a list of three favorite foods and three favorite toys. Write one sentence that lists your favorite foods. Write another sentence that lists your favorite toys.**

1. _Review the sentences to be sure your child has:_
   • _used commas correctly._
   • _written sentences that make sense._

2. _____

## Tips for Your Own Writing: Proofreading ..............

Find a list of things that you have written. Read the list aloud. Did you remember to add commas to separate the items in your list?

*A comma is a pause that clears up confusion in a list.*

41

# 170 Answer Key

# Lesson 19

### Lesson
## 19 Punctuation: Commas in Compound Sentences

*A comma used with **and, but,** or **or** can combine two sentences into one.*

......................... **Did You Know?** .........

**Commas can link two complete sentences together if the words *and, but,* or *or* are used between the sentences.**

> Cats do not like to swim.
> Elephants always bring their trunks.
> Cats do not like to swim, **but** elephants always bring their trunks.

### Show What You Know

**Read each sentence below. Circle the *and, but,* or *or* only if it connects two complete sentences. Then put a slash (/) where a comma should be added.**

1. Leopards have spots /(but) zebras have stripes.

2. Tigers are wild cats /(and) lions are wild cats.

3. Zebras and horses have similar bodies.

4. Do parrots understand what they say /(or) do parrots just copy the sounds of words?

Score: _____    Total Possible: 6

42

---

## Proofread

**Read the story below about people and animals. Four commas are needed where *and, but,* or *or* connects two sentences.**

My mother tells me people are a lot like animals,but they try to be different. Humans do not like to look wrinkled,but elephants are wrinkled all over. People wear black suits, and penguins look like they wear black suits. People carry hairbrushes,but porcupines wear their hairbrushes. Do animals copy people,or do people copy animals?

## Practice

**Think about two things you like to do. Put them together in one sentence. Use a comma and a connecting word.**

> Review the sentences to be sure your child has:
> • used commas correctly with a conjunction.
> • written sentences that make sense.

### Tips for Your Own Writing: Proofreading ..............

Next time you want to combine two sentences, be sure to use **and, but,** or **or.** Place a comma in front of the connecting word.

*Compound sentences can be twice as nice!*

43

---

# Lesson 20

### Lesson
## 20 Review: Commas

**A. Read about Goldilocks below. Add seven commas where they are needed.**

Goldilocks was lost in the forest. She came to a house and went in. She thought that the bowls of porridge were too hot,too cold,and just right. The three chairs felt too hard,too soft,and just right. The beds felt the same way,and Goldilocks fell asleep. The Bear family came home, and Goldilocks ran away. Then Goldilocks visited her grandma,and her grandma told her to write a letter to the Bears.

Score: _____    Total Possible: 7

**B. Add nine commas where they are needed in Goldilocks's letter.**

> June 10,2000
>
> Dear Bear Family,
>
> I got lost in the forest,and I went in your house because I was scared. I am sorry that I ate your porridge,sat in your chairs,and slept in your beds. Will you visit me in Honeyville, Maine? We have lots of fruit,nuts,and honey.
>
> Sincerely,
> Goldilocks

Score: _____    Total Possible: 9

44

---

**C. Read the rhyming sentences below. Then add thirteen commas.**

Papa Bear,Mama Bear,and Baby Bear all rode on a plane. They slept most of the ride,but they awoke in Honeyville,Maine.

Goldilocks met them at the airport,and she grinned from ear to ear. They shook hands with her,smiled at her,and shouted a loud cheer.

At home they ate apples,oranges,berries,nuts,and pears. A new friendship began for a girl and the three bears.

They will remember August 10,2000. They had a nice party,and Goldilocks turned seven!

Score: _____    Total Possible: 13

REVIEW SCORE: _____    REVIEW TOTAL: 29

45

# Lesson 21

### Lesson
## 21 Punctuation: Quotation Marks in Dialogue

*Use quotation marks around words that someone says aloud. It is like the words are surrounded!*

### .................. Did You Know? .......

**Quotation marks go before and after a speaker's words.**

    The reptile roared, **"**I am the great Lizard of Oz!**"**
    The reptile's mother said, **"**You still need to eat your carrots, dear.**"**

### Show What You Know

**Read the sentences below. Circle each speaker's exact words.**

1. (Does anybody have some glue?) asked Humpty Dumpty.

2. (We are so hungry that we could eat a house,) said Hansel and Gretel.

3. Cinderella asked Prince Charming, (Are you a shoe salesman?)

4. (Don't wolf down your food!) exclaimed Little Red Riding Hood.

5. The White Rabbit said, (Digital watches are best.)

Score: _____    Total Possible: 5

46

### Proofread

**Read the story below. Four sentences are missing quotation marks around the speaker's exact words. Circle those words.**

(I am going to the market,) said Mother Pig.

One little piggy fussed, (I want to stay home!)

Another little piggy asked, "Will you please buy me a cookie?"

The next little piggy cried, (I never get anything!)

(Mom, I will be playing baseball!) yelled the last little piggy.

### Practice

**Complete the sentences below by writing what might have been said. Put quotation marks around the words you wrote.**
Sample answers are given.

1. The dragon said, "There is fire in my mouth!"

    *Review the sentences to be sure your child has:*
    • *used quotation marks correctly.*
    • *written sentences that make sense.*

2. _____ "Find my gold!" _____ *yelled the giant.*

### Tips for Your Own Writing: Proofreading ...............

Next time you write a story and your characters say something, use quotation marks around the exact words each speaker says.

*I said, "Use quotation marks. Make people notice what is said!"*

47

.................................................................

# Lesson 22

### Lesson
## 22 Punctuation: Colons in Time

*It is time to tell time! A colon comes in "handy" when telling time!*

### ................... Did You Know? ....................

**Use a colon between the hour and the minutes. This makes it easier to read and understand.**

    The garbage collector gets sad every day at 3:15 p.m. That is when he is down in the dumps.
    The zookeeper was hopping mad at 6:35 p.m. His prize frog was flying a lily pad.

### Show What You Know

**Read these sentences that talk about jobs and time. Put a slash (/) between the hour and the minutes of each time to show where a colon is missing.**

1. The baker quit his job at 8/05 a.m. because he could not make enough dough.

2. The lawyer dressed for court at 9/00 a.m. He wore his best lawsuit.

3. At 4/30 p.m. the mattress salesman was caught lying down on the job.

4. The mechanic fixed the radio at 11/30 a.m. He gave it a tune-up.

Score: _____    Total Possible: 4

48

### Proofread

**Read the poem below. Put in three slashes to show where colons are missing.**

Uncle Goof fixed our roof with a special glue.

A storm began! The glue all ran at 2/22 a.m.!

Grandfather Moore fixed our door at 10/28 p.m.

We've lost our grin. We're still locked in. We must just sit and wait!

Auntie Jinx fixes sinks. She thinks she can repair.

At 6/00 p.m. we all see water squirting in the air!

### Practice

**Write two sentences that have a time in them. Include *a.m.* for a time from midnight to before noon. Include *p.m.* for a time from noon to before midnight.**

    *Review the sentences to be sure your child has:*
1. • *put a colon between the hour and minutes.*
    • *written sentences that make sense.*

2. _____

### Tips for Your Own Writing: Proofreading ...............

Next time you go somewhere, write a note to leave behind. Tell what time you will be back. Remember to put a colon between the hour and the minutes.

*We should give a hand to the colon for helping us tell time!*

49

# Lesson 23

### Lesson
# 23 Punctuation: Periods in Abbreviations

✎ *Some words can be shortened. They end with a period. These words are called abbreviations.*

........................ **Did You Know?** ......................

Some words can be shortened or abbreviated.

**Days of the week and months of the year can be abbreviated only when used in a date. May, June, and July have no abbreviation.**

| | | |
|---|---|---|
| Sunday—**Sun.** | Tuesday—**Tues.** | Thursday—**Thurs.** |
| Monday—**Mon.** | Wednesday—**Wed.** | Friday—**Fri.** |
| | | Saturday—**Sat.** |

| | | |
|---|---|---|
| January—**Jan.** | April—**Apr.** | October—**Oct.** |
| February—**Feb.** | August—**Aug.** | November—**Nov.** |
| March—**Mar.** | September—**Sept.** | December—**Dec.** |

**People's titles can be abbreviated only when used with a name.**

Mister—**Mr.**  Mistress—**Mrs.**  Doctor—**Dr.**

**Types of streets can be abbreviated only when used as part of the name of a street.**

Street—**St.**  Avenue—**Ave.**  Drive—**Dr.**

**Types of measurement can be abbreviated only when used after a number. Most do not need a period.**

pound(s)—**lb(s)**  inch(es)—**in.**  minute(s)—**min**

.......................................................

## Show What You Know

**Circle each word that can be abbreviated.**

(Mister) Tommy Turtle was getting ready for the big race on Runway (Road). He lifted weights that were 2 (pounds) each. He drank 3 (ounces) of juice. Finally, the race began on (Monday), (September) 15, at 9:00 a.m.

Score: _____  Total Possible: 6

50

## Proofread

**Read the story below. Circle the five abbreviations that are missing periods.**

(Mr) Jack Rabbit lived alone at 83 Hutch Ave. His life was good, but he was lonely. Everything changed on (Feb) 13, 2000. Miss Bunny Hare was visiting friends on a nearby street. Jack saw Bunny, and they fell in love. They were married on (Fri) Feb. 14, by (Rev) Cottontail. Bunny carried 3 lbs of carrots for a bouquet. The next day Mr. Jack Rabbit and (Mrs) Bunny Rabbit went on a bunnymoon.

## Practice

**Write a sentence in which you use an abbreviation in your street address. Write another sentence in which you use an abbreviation in your birth date.**

1. _Review the sentences to be sure your child has:_
   _• abbreviated appropriate words and used periods correctly._
   _• written sentences that make sense._

2. _____

## Tips for Your Own Writing: Proofreading ..............

Next time you write a letter to an adult, look at the title of respect. Did you abbreviate it and use a period?

✎ *Abbreviations are short, sweet, and to the point!*

51

......................................................................

# Lesson 24

### Lesson
# 24 Punctuation: Apostrophes in Possessives

✎ *When you want to show others that something belongs to you, use an apostrophe.*

........................ **Did You Know?** ......................

**An apostrophe is used to show that someone owns something.**

**When there is one owner, use 's.**

The prince**'s** golden baseball is kept in a fancy case.

**When there is more than one owner, usually use s'.**

The five royal dog**s'** golden bones were kept in a bowl.

.......................................................

## Show What You Know

**Read the story below. Circle each word that needs an apostrophe to show ownership.**

Lonely, Princess Penny was playing by the (kings) pond. A frog jumped up on a lily pad and croaked, "It is the (kings) pond, but these are all the (frogs) rocks. You may walk on them and play with us."

Princess Penny kissed the (frogs) head, and she turned into a frog!

"Now we can swim in the (kings) pool together!" the frog croaked.

Score: _____  Total Possible: 5

52

## Proofread

**Read the poem below. Circle three words that are missing apostrophes to show ownership.**

The (kings) gold was in the treasury.

The queen's jewels were in a box.

The royal baby lay asleep.

He had the chicken pox.

The (doctors) bottles of medicine

Were kept so nice and cold.

The medicine was special.

The (princes) pox were made of gold.

## Practice

**Write two sentences that show ownership. Do not forget to use 's or s' in each sentence.**

1. _Review the sentences to be sure your child has:_
   _• used 's or s' in each sentence._
   _• written sentences that make sense._

2. _____

## Tips for Your Own Writing: Proofreading ..............

Next time you write about something that is owned, remember to use an apostrophe. Use 's for one owner and s' for more than one owner.

✎ *An apostrophe is proof of ownership. Be sure to use it wisely!*

53

## 25 Punctuation: Underlining Titles

*Underline the titles of books and movies when you are writing their names.*

.............. **Did You Know?** ..............

The titles of books and movies are underlined or put in italics. Underlining helps you find them in the sentence.

After I saw the movie The Little Mermaid, I decided to call my friends and go swimming.

### Show What You Know

**Read the story below. Underline each title.**

The animals were discussing their favorite books and movies. Brandi Bunny loved reading Carrot Seed. Freddie Fox mentioned Chicken Soup with Rice. Then Kitty Cat talked about reading Mouse Soup, but she decided to be quiet when Mortimer Mouse wrinkled his nose. Woody Wolf licked his lips and raved about seeing The Three Little Pigs ten times. He also said that he never stays for the ending. Everyone suddenly was hungry for lunch.

Score: _____ Total Possible: 4

54

### Proofread

**Read each sentence below. Add the missing lines under four book and movie titles.**

**1.** After I saw Aladdin, I wished I had a genie for my friend.

**2.** My dad should read Arthur's Eyes before he gets his new glasses.

**3.** We went to see The Lion King ten times.

**4.** Sharon gave her brother Butch the book Beauty and the Beast for his birthday. He did not laugh.

**5.** Our mail carrier thinks The Jolly Postman is a great book.

### Practice

**Write two sentences about your favorite books and movies. Do not forget to underline the titles.**

1. _Review the sentences to be sure_
   _your child has:_
   • _underlined the titles of books and_
   _movies._
   • _written sentences that make sense._

2. _____

### Tips for Your Own Writing: Proofreading ..............

Look at a book report you have written. Are the titles underlined?

*Language Roundup can help you become a better writer.*

55

## 26 Review: Punctuation

**A. Read the story below. Circle the set of words in five sentences where quotation marks should be used, put three slashes (/) where colons are missing in time, and put a box around three places where periods are missing in abbreviations.**

Mrs Fritzi Frazzle sat working at her computer.

It was already 3/45 p.m., and she had not finished her work.

I will never be done by 6/00 p.m., she said to herself.

Suddenly a spider crawled across her screen.

Eeeek! screamed Fritzi.

Shhh! said the spider. I am looking for flies to go with my burger.

Fritzi left the room. She returned with bug repellent. She sprayed near the computer.

Fritzi happily said, Mrs Fritzi Frazzle's computer has no bugs in it!

She went back to work. She finished at 5/58 p.m. on Mon, August 16.

Score: _____ Total Possible: 11

56

**B. Read the story. Circle the set of words in seven sentences where quotation marks should be used, put two slashes (/) where colons are missing in time, box five words where apostrophes are needed to show ownership, and add one underline under a title.**

Mom, what time is it? asked Buffy.

Her mom answered, It is 2/02. That's two minutes later than the last time you asked.

Will we get to the movie on time? Buffy asked.

Sure, we will. We will meet Mrs. McMann and Muffy at the theater. Muffys brother Murphy may come, too, answered Buffys mom.

Yuk! Murphys manners are disgusting! exclaimed Buffy. She yawned loudly.

They arrived at the movie at 2/15 p.m. Buffy was asleep. Buffys mom woke her, and Buffy dragged herself into the theater.

Everyone sat down. Buffy slept all the way through Sleeping Beauty. She snored.

Mom, said Murphy, Buffys manners are disgusting!

Score: _____ Total Possible: 15

REVIEW SCORE: _____ REVIEW TOTAL: 26

57

# Lesson 27

# Lesson 28

# Lesson 29

## Lesson 29 Usage: Verbs—Was, Were

*Do you know when to use* was *and when to use* were?

### ·····················Did You Know?·····················

*Was* and *were* are verbs. They tell what something or someone is or is like.

Use *was* when you are talking about yourself or one subject.

Jeff **was** a comedian.
I **was** his partner.

Use *were* when you are talking about more than one subject.

Ash and Kawa **were** the funniest.

### Show What You Know

**Read the poem below. If an underlined word is incorrect, cross it out and write the correct word above it.**

We ~~was~~ *were* on the beach.
¹

I ran with my friend Lin.

We <u>were</u> like the wind.
²

Lin stopped to get a shell,

A shell so long and thin.

It ~~were~~ *was* just out of reach.
³

Then the water came.

The shell <u>was</u> out to sea again.
⁴

Score: _____  Total Possible: 2

62

## Proofread

**This story has three mistakes. Draw a line through each incorrect word. Write the correct word above it.**

**Example:** We ~~was~~ *were* on time.

Jared was in the lunchroom. His lunch ~~were~~ *was* at home on the kitchen counter. His parents ~~was~~ *were* at work. Jared ~~were~~ *was* hungry.

## Practice

**Write two sentences telling about what happened when you have forgotten something. Use *was* or *were* in each sentence.**

1. Review the sentences to be sure your child has:
   • used *was* and *were* correctly.
   • written sentences that stick to the topic and make sense.

2. _____

### Tips for Your Own Writing: Proofreading ·············

Read a piece of your writing. Look for the verbs *was* and *were*. Did you use *was* with one subject and *were* with more than one?

*We (was, were) on the move with verbs.*

63

·····································································

# Lesson 30

## Lesson 30 Review: Verbs

**A. Circle the verbs *is* and *are*.**

This (is) a funny bus

With zebra stripes and polka dots,

A driver who (is) Gus,

And a hundred plants in pots.

Gus (is) on a fuzzy seat,

And numbers one through ten

(Are) with her best friend Pete.

Behind (are) letters that look like men.

The bus (is) on its way to school,

Gus seems as happy as can be.

She (is) able to keep her cool.

There (is) so much to see.

Score: _____  Total Possible: 8

**B. Write *is* or *are* in each blank.**

1. A fish ___is___ on another seat.

2. Shapes ___are___ in the aisle.

3. Imagine you ___are___ on the bus.

4. What ___is___ on the seat behind you?

Score: _____  Total Possible: 4

64

**C. Write *was* or *were* in each blank.**

The leaves ___were___ all over the yard. Tom raked them into a
                    ¹

big pile. His little brother ___was___ there. He ___was___ happy.
                             ²               ³

When Tom finished, they ran toward the pile. The pile ___was___ deep.
                                                        ⁴

Then they disappeared. Out they popped! Tom and his brother

___were___ happy.
   ⁵

Score: _____  Total Possible: 5

**D. Read this paragraph. Look for *has* and *have*. If the word is used incorrectly, draw a line through it. Write the correct word above it. There are four mistakes.**

Della and Steve ~~has~~ *have* a plan. They head for the kitchen. Della ~~have~~ *has*

the milk. Steve ~~have~~ *has* the ice cream. Della has the glasses and the spoons.

Della and Steve ~~has~~ *have* chocolate syrup. What are they making?

Score: _____  Total Possible: 4

REVIEW SCORE: _____  REVIEW TOTAL: 21

65

**176**  Answer Key

# Lesson 31

### Lesson 31 Usage: Verbs—Ran, Run

*Both of these words mean "to move fast," but there's a difference!*

...................... **Did You Know?** ......................

*Ran* and *run* are forms of the verb *to run*.

**Use *ran* alone.**

> I **ran** as fast as I could.
> My shadow **ran** behind me.

**Use *run* with *has* or *have*.**

> I **have run** beside a stream.
> The water **has run** along with me.

## Show What You Know

**Write *ran* or *run* in each blank.**

**1.** The ice cream has __run__ down the cone.

**2.** The water __ran__ down the hill.

**3.** The spilled milk __ran__ off the table.

**4.** The fan has __run__ all day.

Score: _____  Total Possible: 4

66

## Proofread

**There are four mistakes in this story. Draw a line through each incorrect word. Write the correct word above it.**

**Example:** The kitten has ~~ran~~ <sup>run</sup> after the toy.

Chris ~~run~~ <sup>ran</sup> to the basketball hoop. Delia and Tomas ran to block her.

Have they ~~ran~~ <sup>run</sup> fast enough? No, Chris throws the ball. It goes through

the hoop. Chris sits down to rest. Tisha has ~~ran~~ <sup>run</sup> onto the court. She will

play for Chris. She has ~~ran~~ <sup>run</sup> all day before. She will not get tired.

## Practice

**Think about animals, people, and things that run. Write one sentence using *ran*. Write another sentence using *has run* or *have run*.**

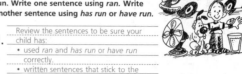

**1.** Review the sentences to be sure your child has:
- used *ran* and *has run* or *have run* correctly.
- written sentences that stick to the topic and make sense.

**2.** _____

## Tips for Your Own Writing: Proofreading

Next time you write about something that runs, look for *ran, has run,* and *have run*. Have you used them correctly?

*We have run out of time for this lesson.*

67

# Lesson 32

### Lesson 32 Usage: Verbs—Did, Done

*Do you know how to use did and done?*

...................... **Did You Know?** ......................

*Did* and *done* are forms of the verb *to do*.

**Use *did* alone.**

> I **did** my homework.
> Pat **did** his, too.

**Use *done* with *has* or *have*.**

> I **have done** all my homework.
> Pat **has done** his, too.

## Show What You Know

**Read the poem below. If the underlined word is used incorrectly, draw a line through it and write the correct word above it.**

Once there was a strange kingdom

With a king who <u>did</u> the farming,

A queen who ~~done~~ <sup>did</sup>[1] the banking,

A prince who <u>did</u> the armor-making,[2]

A princess who ~~done~~ <sup>did</sup>[3] the fishing,

And a sailor who has ~~did~~ <sup>done</sup> the sewing.[4]

[5]

Score: _____  Total Possible: 3

68

## Proofread

**This report has three mistakes. Draw a line through each incorrect word. Write the correct word above it.**

**Example:** We ~~done~~ <sup>did</sup> a good job.

Last month, Nature Club members ~~done~~ <sup>did</sup> a good thing. They cleaned

up the playground. Ten members have ~~did~~ <sup>done</sup> a big poster about recycling.

They ~~done~~ <sup>did</sup> a great job. They will hang the poster in the gym.

## Practice

**Think about a chore you or your friends have done. Write two sentences about it. Be sure to use *did*, *have done*, or *has done* in each sentence.**

**1.** Review the sentences to be sure your child has:
- used *did*, *has done*, and *have done* correctly.
- written sentences that stick to the topic and make sense.

**2.** _____

## Tips for Your Own Writing: Proofreading

The next time you want to write *did* or *done*, make sure *did* is alone. Make sure *done* is with *has* or *have*.

*What have you (did, <u>done</u>) to make your writing better?*

69

# Lesson 33

### Lesson 33 Review: Verbs

**A. Read the sentences below. If the underlined word is incorrect, draw a line through it and write the correct word above it.**

Jeff has ~~ran~~ (run) down the stairs. His dog and cat <u>ran</u> after him. Why
[1]      [2]

have they all ~~ran~~ (run) so fast? Jeff has <u>run</u> to catch the bus. The dog and cat
[3]      [4]

have ~~ran~~ (run) to catch Jeff.
[5]

Score: _____   Total Possible: 3

**B. Read the poem below. Write *did* or *done* in each blank.**

_Did_ you see the sun get ready for bed?
[1]

_Did_ you see the moon sing the sun to sleep?
[2]

My eyes _did_ not close all night.
[3]

But they have _done_ that now.
[4]

Score: _____   Total Possible: 4

**70**

**C. Read this paragraph. Look for *ran* and *run*. If the word is used incorrectly, draw a line through it. Write the correct word above it. There are five mistakes.**

Li and Josh and Ben have ~~ran~~ (run) a race. They ~~run~~ (ran) fast. Josh and Li ran

all the way to the gate and back. Ben did not know how far to go. He

has ~~ran~~ (run) to the gate. He has not ~~ran~~ (run) back. Now they will have to ~~ran~~ (run) the

race again.

Score: _____   Total Possible: 5

**D. Read these sentences. Write the correct word in each blank.**

1. Do you know what Ann has _done_? **(did, done)**

2. She has _run_ into the bushes with her bike. **(ran, run)**

3. April _ran_ into the same bushes with her skates. **(ran, run)**

4. The bushes _did_ not know what to do. **(did, done)**

5. They have _done_ their best to stay away from girls. **(did, done)**

Score: _____   Total Possible: 5

REVIEW SCORE: _____   REVIEW TOTAL: 17

**71**

---

# Lesson 34

### Lesson 34 Usage: Verbs—Went, Gone

*Do you know when to use each of these words?*

#### .................. Did You Know? .........

*Went* and *gone* are forms of the verb *to go*.

**Use *went* alone.**
   Rosa **went** to the snake house.

**Use *gone* with *has* or *have*.**
   Erik **has gone** to the monkey house.

#### Show What You Know

**Read the sentences below. Fill in each blank with *went* or *gone*.**

Mr. Mingle _went_ to the zoo. His students have _gone_
[1]                                      [2]

with him. First they _went_ to see the lions. One lion roared at
[3]

them. Then two owls hooted. Ryan _went_ to see them. The owl he
[4]

found was two feet tall! Now the owl has _gone_ to sleep.
[5]

Score: _____   Total Possible: 5

**72**

#### Proofread

**This note has four mistakes. Draw a line through each incorrect word. Write the correct word above it.**

**Example:** My sister has ~~went~~ (gone) to school.

Dad and I went to my soccer game. John has ~~went~~ (gone) with us. We

have ~~went~~ (gone) to pick up Julie and Justin. Jeremy has not ~~went~~ (gone) with us. He

and Jeff ~~gone~~ (went) to watch a woman juggle. Aunt Judy went with them.

#### Practice

**Write two sentences about a time you went somewhere. Be sure to use *went, has gone,* or *have gone* in each sentence.**

1. Review the sentences to be sure your child has:
   • used *went, has gone,* and *have gone.*
   • written sentences that stick to the topic and make sense.

2. _____

#### Tips for Your Own Writing: Proofreading ............

Read something you have written. Look for the verbs *went* and *gone*. Make sure you have used *went* by itself and *gone* with *has* or *have*.

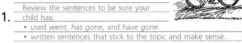

*You have (went, **gone**) through this lesson.*

**73**

# Lesson 35

## Lesson
## 35 Usage: Verbs—Saw, Seen

*See if you can spot the difference between* saw *and* seen.

.................. **Did You Know?**........

*Saw* and *seen* are forms of the verb *to see.*

Use *saw* alone.

I **saw** a black and white whale.

Use *seen* with *has* or *have.*

Beth **has seen** a big, blue whale.

## Show What You Know

**Read the story below. Fill in each blank with** *saw* **or** *seen.*

José and Eva have ___seen___ a fire truck. It raced down the
1

street. They have ___seen___ its red and white lights flash. They stop.
2

Drivers also ___saw___ the truck. They stop their cars. A boy on a
3

bicycle has ___seen___ everyone stop. He stops. José and Eva
4

___saw___ everyone but the fire truck stop.
5

Score: _____ Total Possible: 5

74

## Proofread

**This postcard has two mistakes. Draw a line through each incorrect word. Write the correct word above it.**

**Example:** We ~~seen~~ [saw] Aunt Della at the store.

We are having fun on our trip. I ~~seen~~ [saw]

giant sequoia trees. They are taller than

buildings. The road went through the trunk of one tree. I never ~~seen~~ [saw]

anything like that before. I wish you were here.

## Practice

**Write two sentences about something you have seen. Remember to use** *saw,* *have seen,* **or** *has seen* **in each sentence.**

1. _Review the sentences to be sure your child has:_
   • used *saw, has seen,* and *have seen* correctly.
   • written sentences that stick to the topic and make sense.

2. _____

## Tips for Your Own Writing: Proofreading

Remember that *saw* and *seen* tell about the past. Use *saw* alone. Use *seen* with *has* or *have.*

*Now you have (saw, seen) how to use these words.*

75

# Lesson 36

## Lesson
## 36 Usage: Verbs—Came, Come

*This lesson has come along at just the right time.*

.................. **Did You Know?** ..................

*Came* and *come* are forms of the verb *to come.*

Use *came* alone.

The children **came** to Ling's party.

Use *come* with *has* or *have.*
Use *has come* with one subject.

Deb **has come** to the party dressed as a bee.

Use *have come* when you talk about more than one subject.

Rosa and Jake **have come** dressed like crayons.

## Show What You Know

**Everything lives somewhere. The sentences below match animals with their homes. Fill in each blank with** *came* **or** *come.*

1. The busy bee ___came___ to the hive.

2. The noisy blue jay ___came___ to the nest.

3. The black bear has ___come___ to the cave.

Score: _____ Total Possible: 3

76

## Proofread

**There are three mistakes in this note. Draw a line through each incorrect word. Write the correct word above it.**

**Example:** She ~~come~~ [came] on time.

I'm glad you ~~come~~ [came] to my party. You have always ~~came~~ [come] in neat

costumes. I liked your funny scarecrow costume. I did not know your

crow ~~come~~ [came] from a store. My cat is sorry he tried to

eat your crow!

## Practice

**Choose two words from the list below and write two sentences. Be sure to use** *came,* *has come,* **or** *have come* **in each sentence.**

| movie theater | park | pool | grocery store | circus |
| friend's house | dentist | library | post office | pet store |

1. _Review the sentences to be sure your child has:_
   • used *came, has come,* and *have come* correctly.
   • written sentences that include two words from the list and that make sense.

2. _____

## Tips for Your Own Writing: Proofreading

Next time you write about a trip, look for the words *came* and *come.* Make sure you have used *came* by itself and *come* with *has* or *have.*

*This lesson has come to an end.*

77

# Lesson 37

Lesson
# 37 Review: Verbs

**A. Read the story below. Write *came* or *come* in each blank.**

The sea came (1) to the beach.

It has come (2) as far as it can reach.

Do you think it came (3) to find a shell?

Maybe it has come (4) with a tale to tell.

**Score: ______ Total Possible: 4**

**B. Read the story below. Write *saw* or *seen* in each blank.**

I went to the circus. I saw (1) a clown riding a mule. Then I noticed something funny. I saw (2) two monkeys riding on the clown. I have not seen (3) that before! Then I saw (4) four doves riding on the monkeys. Were eight fleas riding on the doves?

**Score: ______ Total Possible: 4**

78

**C. Read the story below. Write *went* or *gone* in each blank.**

Amy has gone (1) to the park. She wants to climb the rock mountain. Rob and Pete went (2) with her. They have gone (3) to slide and swing. Do you think they went (4) the short way? They would have had to walk through the mud.

**Score: ______ Total Possible: 4**

**D. Look at the words in each column. Draw a line between pairs that make sense. Use each pair only once.** Sample answers are given.

| | |
|---|---|
| Ted and Liz have | went to see the movie star. |
| My brother | ran to get the mail. |
| Tess | gone to feed the ducks. |
| Gilbert has | come home early today. |
| Morgan | run a hundred miles. |
| I think Carmen has | came to the park with us. |

**Score: ______ Total Possible: 6**

**REVIEW SCORE: ______ REVIEW TOTAL: 18**

79

# Lesson 38

Lesson
# 38 Usage: Adjectives That Compare

*These words can add some sparkle to your writing.*

## Did You Know?

**We can use words to describe and compare things. Add *-er* to an adjective when you compare two things. Add *-est* when you compare three or more things.**

That airplane is **fast.**
This airplane is **faster** than that one.
This airplane is the **fastest** of all.

## Show What You Know

**This chart is not complete. Fill in the empty boxes with the correct word.**

| | | |
|---|---|---|
| short | shorter | shortest |
| large | larger | largest |
| bright | brighter | brightest |
| long | longer | longest |
| high | higher | highest |

**Score: ______ Total Possible: 6**

80

## Proofread

**This report has four mistakes. Draw a line through each incorrect word. Write the correct word above it.**

**Example:** Ben is ~~shortest~~ shorter than Tim.

A gorilla is big. A chimp is ~~smallest~~ smaller than a gorilla. A tiger is ~~strong~~ stronger than a lion. Did you know that tigers do not live in Africa? A man ~~smart~~ smarter than my brother told me that. He also told me that a cheetah is the ~~faster~~ fastest animal of all.

## Practice

**Use the words from the box on page 80 to compare something. Write two sentences. Be sure to write whole sentences, like this one.**

Becky's bike is **taller** than Seth's. My bike is the **tallest** one at the bike rack.

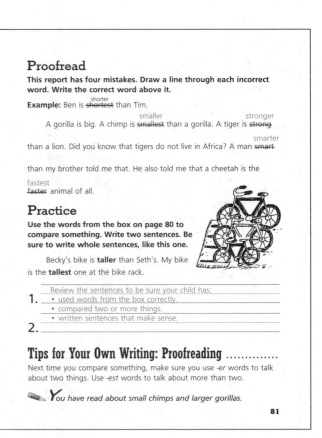

1. Review the sentences to be sure your child has:
   - used words from the box correctly.
   - compared two or more things.
   - written sentences that make sense.
2.

## Tips for Your Own Writing: Proofreading

Next time you compare something, make sure you use *-er* words to talk about two things. Use *-est* words to talk about more than two.

*You have read about small chimps and larger gorillas.*

81

# Lesson 39

## Lesson 39 Usage: Homophones–To/Too/Two

✎ *This lesson will help you keep these three little words straight.*

### ....................... Did You Know? .......................

Some words sound alike even when they mean different things and have different spellings.

The word *to* has two meanings. It can mean "toward." *To* is also used before a verb.

> I found a penny when I walked **to** the store.
> I want **to** read that book.

The word *too* has two meanings. It can mean "also." *Too* can also be used to mean "very" or "more than enough."

> Ike found a penny, **too**.
> I am **too** tired to watch the movie.

The word *two* means the number 2.

> Paul found **two** pennies.

### Show What You Know

**Read the paragraph below. Fill in each blank with *to*, *too*, or *two*.**

My brother is learning ___to___ juggle. He started with
                                 1
___two___ balls. I asked him ___to___ teach me, ___too___ .
    2                             3                   4

Score: _____    Total Possible: 4

82

---

## Proofread

This note has four mistakes. Draw a line through each incorrect word. Write the correct word above it.

**Example:** I'm not ~~to~~ (too) sleepy.

Julie asked me to come ~~too~~ (to) her party. She is going ~~two~~ (to) have ~~to~~ (two)

cakes and ~~too~~ (two) kinds of ice cream. Jill is coming, too. It will be so much

fun. I cannot wait to go.

## Practice

Write two sentences. One should be about *two* of something. The other should tell about going to a place you like. Try to use *too* in one of the sentences, too!

1. _____
   Review the sentences to be sure your child has:
   • used *two* and *to* (and *too* if it fits in) correctly.
   • written sentences that make sense.

2. _____

## Tips for Your Own Writing: Proofreading ..............

Read a piece of your writing. Look for the words *to*, *too*, and *two*. Have you used *two* when you are talking about a number? Have you used *too* to mean "also," "very," or "more than enough"? Have you used *to* before verbs or to mean "toward"?

✎ *You have had more than (to, too, __two__) chances (__to__, too, two) use these same-sounding words.*

83

---

# Lesson 40

## Lesson 40 Review: Adjectives, Homophones

**A. Read the poem below. Write *to*, *too*, or *two* in each blank.**

This morning it started ___to___ rain.

The ___two___ of us were sad.

We couldn't go ___to___ our baseball game.

"That's ___too___ bad," said Dad.

Score: _____    Total Possible: 4

**B. Fill in the blanks to complete the chart.**

| slow | slower | slowest |
|------|--------|---------|
| fast | faster | fastest |
| dark | darker | darkest |
| little | littler | littlest |
| tall | taller | tallest |
| short | shorter | shortest |

Score: _____    Total Possible: 10

84

---

**C. Finish the comparisons by writing the correct word in each blank.**

1. An eagle is ___bigger___ than a sparrow. (**big, bigger, biggest**)

2. A dinosaur might have been the ___heaviest___ animal of all time. (**heavy, heavier, heaviest**)

3. A bus has ___larger___ seats than a car. (large, larger, largest)

4. The night sky is ___darker___ than the day sky. (**dark, darker, darkest**)

5. That is a ___soft___ feather pillow. (**soft, softer, softest**)

6. This oak tree is the ___oldest___ one on my block. (**old, older, oldest**)

7. The ocean is ___colder___ than the pool. (**cold, colder, coldest**)

8. Monday was ___hot___ . (**hot, hotter, hottest**)

Score: _____    Total Possible: 8

REVIEW SCORE: _____    REVIEW TOTAL: 22

85

# Lesson 41

### Lesson
# 41 Usage: Plurals That Add -s

✏️ *Changing a noun from one to more than one is easy!*

........................ **Did You Know?** ........................

Nouns are words that name objects. You can make most nouns mean "more than one" by adding *-s* to the end of the word. This is called a plural noun.

one shoe    two shoe**s**
one balloon    five balloon**s**

## Show What You Know

Write each word so that it means more than one.

**1.** animal    animals          **6.** bat    bats

**2.** sister    sisters          **7.** book    books

**3.** kitten    kittens          **8.** toy    toys

**4.** truck    trucks            **9.** dog    dogs

**5.** backpack    backpacks      **10.** river    rivers

Score: _____    Total Possible: 10

86

## Proofread

There are three mistakes in this invitation. Draw a line through each incorrect word. Write the correct word above it.

**Example:** I saw two ~~dog~~. (dogs)

Please come to my party. We will play ~~game~~ (games) and have fun. We will eat ~~hot dog~~ (hot dogs), ~~chip~~ (chips), and birthday cake. The party will last two hours. Hope you can come!

## Practice

Fill in the blanks to make a list about the picture. Use the words to write two sentences about the picture.

one    clown          two    shoes    with polka dots

three    balls         four    buttons

**1.** Review the sentences to be sure your child has:
 • used words from the list correctly.
 • written sentences that make sense.

**2.** _____

## Tips for Your Own Writing: Proofreading

When you write a word that means more than one, check to see that you have added *-s*.

✏️ *Did you see that this lesson uses two pages?*

87

---

# Lesson 42

### Lesson
# 42 Usage: Plurals That Add -es

✏️ *Watch how the nouns end in this lesson.*

........................ **Did You Know?** ........................

To make some nouns mean more than one, you add *-es*. Add *-es* to words ending in *sh*, *ch*, *x*, *s*, and *z*.

one brush    two brush**es**
one dress    two dress**es**

## Show What You Know

Write each word so that it means more than one.

**1.** brush    brushes          **6.** dress    dresses

**2.** ax    axes                **7.** flash    flashes

**3.** box    boxes              **8.** lunch    lunches

**4.** bench    benches          **9.** dish    dishes

**5.** class    classes          **10.** fox    foxes

Score: _____    Total Possible: 10

88

## Proofread

This poem has two mistakes. Can you fix them? Cross out each incorrect word. Write the correct word above it.

**Example:** There are three ~~box~~ (boxes) on the table.

I was lunching one day up at Trish's
When an elf came and offered me ~~wish~~ (wishes).

I looked at my peas

Said "Thank you" and "Please,
Use my wishes to clean up these ~~dish~~ (dishes)!"

## Practice

Choose two words that mean more than one from the list on page 88. Use each word in a sentence.

**1.** Review the sentences to be sure your child has:
 • used words from the list correctly.
 • written sentences that make sense.

**2.** _____

## Tips for Your Own Writing: Proofreading

Remember: When you want to make a word mean more than one, look at the end of the word. If it ends in *s*, *x*, *z*, *sh*, or *ch*, add *-es* to the end.

✏️ *Do you need to wear glasses to do this lesson?*

89

# Lesson 43

### Lesson 43 Review: Plurals

**A. Add -s to make each word mean "more than one." Write the word on the line.**

1. ball _____balls_____

2. bat _____bats_____

3. shoe _____shoes_____

4. glove _____gloves_____

5. field _____fields_____

Score: _____ Total Possible: 5

**B. Add -es to make each word mean "more than one." Write the word on the line.**

1. brush _____brushes_____

2. box _____boxes_____

3. sash _____sashes_____

4. mess _____messes_____

5. lunch _____lunches_____

Score: _____ Total Possible: 5

90

**C. Fill in the blanks. Add -s or -es to the word in parentheses ( ).**

1. Aunt Min sent me a box of ___paints___. (paint)

2. She also sent two new ___brushes___. (brush)

3. My brother got ten ___markers___. (marker)

4. We have made a lot of ___pictures___. (picture)

5. We have made a lot of ___messes___, too. (mess)

6. I am sending two ___paintings___ to Aunt Min. (painting)

7. One is a girl holding two ___bunches___ of flowers. (bunch)

8. One is a girl running the ___bases___ on a baseball field. (base)

9. The paintings of the ___girls___ are both of me. (girl)

10. I like to do a lot of ___things___. (thing)

Score: _____ Total Possible: 10

REVIEW SCORE: _____ REVIEW TOTAL: 20

91

# Lesson 44

### Lesson 44 Usage: Contractions

This lesson is about taking shortcuts when you speak and write.

...................... **Did You Know?** ......................

Sometimes we put two words together to make one shorter word. The shorter word is called a contraction.

   is not—isn't     are not—aren't
   was not—wasn't    were not—weren't

When we make contractions by using *not*, we leave out the *o* in *not* and put an apostrophe (') in its place.

.........................................................

#### Show What You Know

Write the contraction on the line.

1. is not _____isn't_____

2. are not _____aren't_____

3. was not _____wasn't_____

4. were not _____weren't_____

Write the correct contraction in each sentence.

1. Amy _____isn't_____ going to the party. (isn't, aren't)

2. The boys _____weren't_____ happy about the team. (wasn't, weren't)

Score: _____ Total Possible: 6

92

#### Proofread

Find the four mistakes in this paragraph. Draw a line through each incorrect word. Write the correct word above it.

**Example:** They ~~arent~~ *aren't* here today.

   The clouds were big yesterday. But they ~~werent~~ *weren't* very fluffy. Bill ~~wasnot~~ *wasn't* here to see them. Bill is here today, ~~is'nt~~ *isn't* he? ~~Are'nt~~ *Aren't* he and Les over by the fence? No, that's someone else.

#### Practice

Write one sentence about someone you know. Use *isn't* or *aren't*. Write another sentence about you or a friend. Use *wasn't* or *weren't*.

**Examples:** My brother isn't tall.
          I wasn't tired.

1. _____Review the sentences to be sure your child has:_____
    • used contractions correctly and placed the apostrophes correctly.
    • written sentences that stick to the topic and make sense.

2. _____

#### Tips for Your Own Writing: Proofreading .............

Look at a story you have written. Find the words *isn't, aren't, wasn't,* and *weren't*. Have you spelled them correctly? Is the apostrophe (') in the right place?

*Forming a contraction isn't a mystery if you know the rule.*

93

# Lesson 45

## Lesson 45 Usage: Isn't, Aren't

*Here are two words you use every day. Do you use them correctly?*

.......................... **Did You Know?** ......................

*Isn't* and *aren't* are contractions. Use *isn't* when you talk about one.

> Rachel **isn't** eating her peas.

Use *aren't* when you talk about more than one.

> Sue and Ann **aren't** eating their peas, either.

....................................................

### Show What You Know

**Read the story below. Fill in the blanks with *isn't* or *aren't*.**

My grandmother ___isn't___ like most grandmothers. My brother
                     1

and I ___aren't___ allowed to eat cookies before supper. We
             2

___aren't___ allowed to stay up late. But my grandmother takes me to
    3

the park. She lets me play on the really big slide. She ___isn't___
                                                            4

supposed to do that. ___Isn't___ my grandmother a lot of fun?
                          5

Score: _____    Total Possible: 5

94

## Proofread

**Read Jill's report about two animals she saw at the zoo. Draw a line through each incorrect word. Write the correct word above it. There are three mistakes.**

**Example:** That book ~~aren't~~ isn't about animals.

Lions and tigers ~~isn't~~ aren't the same. A lion's mane ~~isnt~~ isn't on a tiger. A tiger's stripes ~~isn't~~ aren't on a lion. A lion is a cat, and a tiger is a cat. But a tiger isn't a lion.

## Practice

**Write two sentences about something that was not done right. Use *isn't* and *aren't*.**
**Examples:** My toast isn't dark.
My eggs aren't ready.

1. _____
   Review the sentences to be sure your child has:
   • used *isn't* and *aren't* correctly and have placed the apostrophes correctly.
2. _____
   • written sentences that stick to the topic and make sense.

## Tips for Your Own Writing: Proofreading

When you write *isn't* or *aren't*, remember to put the apostrophe (') in the right place. Have you used *isn't* to talk about one? Have you used *aren't* to talk about more than one?

*Isn't a contraction a shortcut to writing two words?*

95

---

# Lesson 46

## Lesson 46 Usage: Wasn't, Weren't

*What is the difference between these words?*

.......................... **Did You Know?** ......................

*Wasn't* and *weren't* are two more contractions.

Use *wasn't* when you talk about one.

> Tom **wasn't** on the bus.

Use *weren't* when you talk about more than one and with the word *you*.

> **Weren't** Lee and Min the last to get on?
> You **weren't** the last one.

....................................................

### Show What You Know

**Read the story below. Write *wasn't* or *weren't* in the blanks.**

My brother Mike ___wasn't___ eating his peas. He put them in
                      1

the flowerpot. Mom noticed. Peas ___weren't___ part of her ivy plant.
                                      2

Then Mike tried to make the dog eat his peas. The dog ___wasn't___
                                                            3

happy. I hoped Mike's peas ___weren't___ about to land on my plate!
                                4

Score: _____    Total Possible: 4

96

## Proofread

**This thank-you note has three mistakes. Draw a line through each incorrect word. Write the correct word above it.**

**Example:** You ~~wasn't~~ weren't late.

Dear Aunt Jo,

Thank you for taking me to the circus. ~~Weren't~~ Wasn't it fun? I ~~werent~~ wasn't really scared. I knew those two men weren't going to fall. You ~~wasn't~~ weren't scared, were you?

Love,

Ashley

## Practice

**Write two sentences. Use *wasn't* or *weren't* in each sentence.**
**Examples:** The pool wasn't open.
The children weren't happy.

1. _____
   Review the sentences to be sure your child has:
   • used *wasn't* and *weren't* correctly and have placed the apostrophes in the correct location.
2. _____
   • written sentences that make sense.

## Tips for Your Own Writing: Proofreading

Check your writing for the words *wasn't* and *weren't*. Have you used *wasn't* to talk about one? Have you used *weren't* with the word *you* and to talk about more than one?

*I (wasn't, weren't) finished using these contractions.*

97

# Lesson 47

### Lesson
## 47 Review: Contractions

**A. Read the story below. Write *isn't* or *aren't* in each blank.**

My dog Bo _____isn't_____<sub>1</sub> a collie.

He _____isn't_____<sub>2</sub> a husky, either. My

father and mother _____aren't_____<sub>3</sub> sure what he is. He likes to run. He

chases the ball I throw. He _____isn't_____<sub>4</sub> ready to stop when I am.

Score: _____    Total Possible: 4

**B. Lucy wrote about "Jack and the Beanstalk." She could not remember when to use *wasn't* and *weren't*. Help her out. Write the correct word in each blank.**

Jack and his mom _____weren't_____<sub>1</sub> rich. They needed to sell their

cow. Jack _____wasn't_____<sub>2</sub> supposed to trade the cow for three beans.

His mom _____wasn't_____<sub>3</sub> happy when he came home with beans.

_____Weren't_____<sub>4</sub> they surprised when a big beanstalk grew!

Score: _____    Total Possible: 4

98

**C. Read this story. Look for *isn't*, *aren't*, *wasn't*, and *weren't*. Find the six mistakes. Draw a line through each incorrect word. Write the correct word above it.**

The rabbits ~~are'nt~~ [aren't] in the cage. Where did they go? I hope Nell is

giving them a bath. They ~~werent~~ [weren't] clean enough. ~~Arn't~~ [Isn't] she supposed to

clean the cage, too? Yes, but aren't Patrick and Janice going to help?

They ~~isn't~~ [aren't] home. This ~~isno't~~ [isn't] fair. Oh, look! We have six clean rabbits. I

guess I will clean the cage. The rabbits ~~isn't~~ [aren't] going to get dirty again.

Score: _____    Total Possible: 6

**D. Finish these sentences with *isn't* or *aren't*.**

1. My name _____isn't_____ Sal.

2. My eyes _____aren't_____ blue.

3. My song _____isn't_____ long.

4. My stories _____aren't_____ true.

Score: _____    Total Possible: 4

REVIEW SCORE: _____    REVIEW TOTAL: 18

99

..........

# Lesson 48

### Lesson
## 48 Usage: Adding *-ed*

*You can change the meaning of a verb by adding -ed.*

......................... **Did You Know?** .........................

To make most verbs tell about the past, you add *-ed* to the end of the word.

want    want**ed**
lift    lift**ed**

If the action word ends in *e*, add just *-d*.

like    like**d**
use    use**d**

## Show What You Know

**Fill in the blanks with the verb that shows that the action happened in the past.**

1. Min _____kicked_____ the ball to Lee. **(kick, kicked)**

2. Jeff _____wanted_____ to play, too. **(want, wanted)**

3. Lee and Min _____called_____ him over. **(call, called)**

4. Jeff _____rushed_____ over. **(rush, rushed)**

5. They all _____used_____ the ball. **(use, used)**

Score: _____    Total Possible: 5

100

## Proofread

This story has six mistakes. Draw a line through each incorrect word. Write the correct word above it.

**Example:** I ~~talk~~ [talked] to my friend last night.

On Friday, Amy ~~skate~~ [skated] with Anna and April. They are good friends.

Amy ~~ask~~ [asked] Anna and April to skate next to her. They ~~look~~ [looked] like sisters. Amy

turned around and ~~skate~~ [skated] backwards. Anna ~~twirl~~ [twirled] April wanted to twirl.

She fell down instead. Amy ~~help~~ [helped] April get up.

## Practice

Write two sentences about something you did this week. Use action words with *-ed* on the end.

1. _____Review the sentences to be sure your child has:_____
   _• added -ed to verbs to form the past tense correctly._
2. _• written sentences that stick to the topic and make sense._

## Tips for Your Own Writing: Proofreading

Next time you write about something that happened in the past, check your verbs. Have you spelled them correctly? Did you add *-ed*? If the word ended in *e*, did you add only the *-d*?

*We worked hard adding the -ed ending.*

101

# Lesson 49

## Lesson 49

### Lesson 49 Usage: Adding -s

*Say this three times: She sells seashells.*

........................ **Did You Know?** ......................

**Action verbs that tell what one subject is doing end in *s*.**

She **runs**. He **runs**. It **runs**. The dog **barks**.

**Action verbs that tell what more than one subject is doing do not end in *s*.**

The dogs **bark**.

**Action verbs that tell about you, we, or they do not end in *s*, either.**

You **run**. We **run**. They **run**.

........................................................................

### Show What You Know

Fill in the blanks with the correct form of the verb. Draw a circle around the person or thing the verb tells about.

**1.** (Jan) _____kicks_____ the ball. (**kick, kicks**)

**2.** The (ball) _____rolls_____ into the bushes. (**roll, rolls**)

**3.** (Ben) _____pulls_____ and tugs, but the ball is stuck. (**pull, pulls**)

**4.** (Jan) _____tugs_____ on the ball until it pops free. (**tug, tugs**)

Score: _____ Total Possible: 8

102

### Proofread

There are three mistakes in this report. Draw a line through each incorrect word. Write the correct word above it.

**Example:** I ~~walks~~ *walk* to school.

I live in a noisy house. My brother yells. The dogs ~~barks~~ *bark*. The cat ~~say~~ *says* meow, meow, meow. Even the bird ~~talk~~ *talks*. She says "good morning" to me every night.

### Practice

Look at the picture. Write two sentences about what the children are doing. Use action words.

**1.** *Review the sentences to be sure your child has:*
• *used singular and plural verbs correctly.*
• *written sentences that stick to the topic and make sense.*

**2.** _____

### Tips for Your Own Writing: Proofreading .............

Look at a piece of your writing. Check your action verbs. Do they end in *-s* when you talk about one person or thing? How do they end when you talk about more than one person or thing, or about you, we, or they?

*We write the answers. Our teacher checks them.*

103

---

# Lesson 50

## Lesson 50

### Lesson 50 Review: Adding -ed/-s

**A. Fill in each blank. Show that the action has already happened.**

**1.** Last week, Ben _____played_____ his drum. (**play**)

**2.** He _____banged_____ on it with sticks. (**bang**)

**3.** The neighbors _____covered_____ their ears. (**cover**)

**4.** Ben's mom _____closed_____ her door. (**close**)

Score: _____ Total Possible: 4

**B. Fill in each blank. Show that the action is happening right now.**

**1.** Roger _____hunts_____ for his homework (**hunt**)

**2.** He _____sees_____ many things, but not that. (**see**)

**3.** His baseball bat _____sits_____ in the corner. (**sit**)

**4.** His hat _____hangs_____ on the light. (**hang**)

Score: _____ Total Possible: 4

104

**C. Choose the correct form of the word. Write your answer in each blank.**

**1.** Cinderella _____works_____ hard. (**work, works**)

**2.** She _____cleans_____ dishes all day. (**clean, cleans**)

**3.** She _____sews_____ torn clothing late at night. (**sew, sews**)

**4.** The mice _____help_____ Cinderella a little. (**help, helps**)

**5.** Her mean sisters _____played_____ while she worked. (**plays, played**)

**6.** Cinderella _____thinks_____ about the Prince's ball. (**think, thinks**)

Score: _____ Total Possible: 6

**D. This recipe tells how to make breakfast. Look at the underlined words. If the wrong verb is used, cross it out. Write the correct verb above it. There are five mistakes.**

First you ~~opens~~ *open* the box. Then you ~~pours~~ *pour* out the cereal. Oops, I forgot. You _need_ a bowl. My mother ~~add~~ *adds* milk for me. I ~~spills~~ *spill* the milk when I pour it. Then I ~~eats~~ *eat* my breakfast.

Score: _____ Total Possible: 5

REVIEW SCORE: _____ REVIEW TOTAL: 19

105

# Lesson 51

### Lesson
# 51 Usage: Using *I*

*You and I will learn about the word I.*

...................... **Did You Know?** ......................

When you talk about what you do or who you are, use the word *I*.

Always write *I* with a capital letter. *I* is a pronoun that is used as a subject.

**I** helped my mom today.

When you talk about yourself and someone else, speak of yourself last.

**Mom and I** planted flowers outside.

## Show What You Know

Finish this story. Write *I* in the blanks. Then read each sentence to a friend.

Mom asked me to show her how a robot acts. __I__₁ marched

across the room. Then she asked me to work hard like a robot. __I__₂

put my toys away. __I__₃ also gave Mom my dirty shirts and socks.

__I__₄ think Mom tricked me into cleaning my room!

Score: _____    Total Possible: 4

106

## Proofread

This journal entry has three mistakes. Cross out each mistake. Write the correct word or words above it.

**Example:** Mom and ~~me~~ ᴵ ate breakfast.

Dad and I
~~I and Dad~~ were busy today. We worked outside. ᴵ pulled weeds and

planted flowers. Pam came over, too. Dad, Pam, and I watered the new

plants. Pam and I got dirty. ᴵ had lots of fun.

## Practice

Write two sentences to tell about something you and someone else did.

1. _Review the sentences to be sure your child has:_
   • _used I correctly and capitalized it._
   • _written sentences that stick to the topic and make sense._

2. _____

## Tips for Your Own Writing: Proofreading ..............

Look at a piece of writing in which you wrote about yourself. Circle each *I*. Check to see whether you used it correctly.

*I hope you and I are getting the hang of this.*

107

---

# Lesson 52

### Lesson
# 52 Usage: Using *Me*

*Knowing when to use me can be a little tricky. This lesson will help.*

...................... **Did You Know?** ......................

Sometimes when you talk about yourself, you are not the main person the sentence is about. In this case, use the word *me*. *Me* is a pronoun, just like *I* is.

Barry walked with **me** to the pool.

When you talk about yourself and someone else, speak of yourself last.

Kandi came with **Barry and me**.

## Show What You Know

Fill in each blank with the correct word or words.

1. My brother Alex chased __me__ through the house. (**I, me**)

2. He wanted __me__ to take out the trash. (**I, me**)

3. Mom told __Alex and me__ to stop running through the house. (**me and Alex, Alex and me**)

4. So I ran outside, and Alex kept chasing __me__! (**I, me**)

Score: _____    Total Possible: 4

108

## Proofread

Find the four mistakes in this secret story. Draw a line through the incorrect word or words. Write the correct word or words above.

**Example:** They were waiting for ~~me and Jilly~~. Jilly and me

Dad and I have a secret. It is just between Dad and ~~I~~. me Dad told it to
me
~~I~~ last night. He said he knew I would not tell. He said it was only for
him and me                    Dad and me
~~me and him~~. Mom will want ~~me and Dad~~ to tell her. We cannot tell

Mom. The secret is about her birthday present.

## Practice

Write two sentences about times when someone did something for you. Be sure to use *me* in each one.

**Example:** My grandmother bought me a piece of apple pie.

1. _Review the sentences to be sure your child has:_
   • _used me correctly._
   • _written sentences that stick to the topic and make sense._

2. _____

## Tips for Your Own Writing: Proofreading ..............

The next time you write about something that happened to you, use the word *me*. Use *I* when you are the one doing or being something. When you talk about yourself and a friend, speak of yourself last.

*Sometimes I am confused when I talk about (I, me).*

109

# Lesson 53

Lesson
## 53 Review: *I/Me*

**A. Read this paragraph. Write *I* or *me* in each blank.**

Pam and ___I___ went to the park. She and ___I___
                1                                    2

wanted to sled down the hill. Pam went first. She waited for ___me___
                                                                3

at the bottom. She and ___I___ walked up the hill together. Next
                          4

time she and ___I___ rode together. The sled went very fast with
                5

Pam and ___me___ on it.
           6

Score: _____   Total Possible: 6

**B. Find the three mistakes in this story. Draw a line through the incorrect word. Write the correct word above it.**

**Example:** They called ~~I~~ me on the phone.

                I
~~Me~~ like to sleep with my teddy bear. He makes

                                        me
me feel safe at night. The dark does not bother ~~I~~

when Teddy is watching. I do not tell my

friends about my teddy. I think they might laugh. Mom

        me
told ~~I~~ she used to sleep with a teddy bear.

Score: _____   Total Possible: 3

**110**

---

**C. Read each sentence. Choose the correct answer and write it in the blank.**

1. Both ___Dad and I___ wanted to go to the library.
   **(Dad and me, Dad and I)**

2. ___I___ needed a book for a book report. **(I, me)**

3. My little sister Becky wanted to come with ___Dad and me___.
   **(me and Dad, Dad and me)**

4. ___Becky and I___ told Dad we should go to the children's
   section. **(Becky and I, I and Becky)**

5. I found a book ___I___ liked. **(I, me)**

6. Dad helped ___me___ check it out. **(I, me)**

7. ___I___ ran to the car with my book. **(I, me)**

8. Becky ran behind ___me___. **(I, me)**

Score: _____   Total Possible: 8

REVIEW SCORE: _____   REVIEW TOTAL: 17

**111**

.................................................

# Lesson 54

Lesson
## 54 Grammar: Common Nouns

*Carefully study the "Parts of Speech" before making one!*

### ............. Did You Know? .............

**Nouns are parts of speech. Common nouns name any person, place, thing, or idea.**

Gabby is a (crow) who loves to shop. She sits on the telephone (wire) and "caws" the shopping (channel) Gabby has bought so many (things) that her (tree) is too crowded.

### Show What You Know

**Look for the common nouns in this poem. Underline each one. You should find fourteen.**

Penny was a small pack <u>rat</u>,

Who collected many <u>things</u>

Like fuzzy <u>hats</u>, a <u>thermostat</u>,

Two bouncy <u>springs</u>, ten shiny <u>rings</u>,

A frying <u>pan</u>, an old tin <u>can</u>,

A ragged <u>map</u>, a bottle <u>cap</u>,

A Chinese <u>fan</u>, a little <u>van</u>,

A broken <u>strap</u>, and new <u>mousetrap</u>!

Score: _____   Total Possible: 14

**112**

---

### Practice

**Read the paragraph below. Write a common noun in each blank.**
Sample answers are given.

I really wanted to have a ___pet___
                             1

I asked my ___mother___ whether I could
             2

have one. I had to save money. Finally I went

to the ___store___ and bought a ___cat___. I fed it lots of
         3                          4

___fish___, and my ___cat___ began to grow and grow.
   5                 6

### Revise

**Write a sentence about another pet. Underline the common nouns.**
A sample answer is given.

___My <u>puppy</u> ate <u>dinner</u>.___

**Reread your sentence. Change some of the common nouns to make the sentence funny. Rewrite the sentence.**
A sample answer is given.

___My <u>puppy</u> ate my <u>slippers</u>.___

### Tips for Your Own Writing: Proofreading .............

Next time you write a letter, reread it. Can you find the common nouns? Ask someone to help you make sure you found all the common nouns.

*A noun will tell you what all the fuss is about.*

**113**

# Lesson 55

### Lesson
## 55 Grammar: Common and Proper Nouns

*There is a proper way to name some parts of speech. My teacher, Mr. Gorman, told me that.*

...................... **Did You Know?** ......................

A <u>common noun</u> names any person, place, thing, or idea.

A <u>proper noun</u> names a special person, a special place, or a special thing. A proper noun begins with a capital letter.

Dr. Penn went to examine the piglets at Old McPorker's Farm. He prescribed "Babe's Sunscreen Oinkment" for their bad sunburn. They had been "bacon" in the sun!

### Show What You Know

**Read the poem. Circle every proper noun. You should find seven.**

At (Zelda's Zany Zoo)

The animals were sick.

(Cameron Camel) lost his hump.

(Presley Python) ate a stick.

(Zelda) quickly made a call

To (Little Clinic) in (L.A.)

(Dr. Little) flew out fast.

He came that very day.

Score: _____ Total Possible: 7

114

## Practice

**Read the paragraph below. Write a proper noun in each blank.** Sample answers are given.

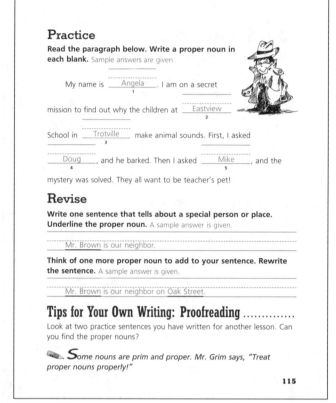

My name is ___Angela___ . I am on a secret
　　　　　　　　 1

mission to find out why the children at ___Eastview___
　　　　　　　　　　　　　　　　　　　　　　　2

School in ___Trotville___ make animal sounds. First, I asked
　　　　　　　3

___Doug___ , and he barked. Then I asked ___Mike___ , and the
　　4　　　　　　　　　　　　　　　　　　　5

mystery was solved. They all want to be teacher's pet!

## Revise

**Write one sentence that tells about a special person or place. Underline the proper noun.** A sample answer is given.

Mr. Brown is our neighbor.

**Think of one more proper noun to add to your sentence. Rewrite the sentence.** A sample answer is given.

Mr. Brown is our neighbor on Oak Street.

### Tips for Your Own Writing: Proofreading .............

Look at two practice sentences you have written for another lesson. Can you find the proper nouns?

*Some nouns are prim and proper. Mr. Grim says, "Treat proper nouns properly!"*

115

---

# Lesson 56

### Lesson
## 56 Grammar: Pronouns

*Talk about yourself. Did you use the word I to refer to yourself? Great! Then you already know something about pronouns.*

...................... **Did You Know?** ......................

Pronouns take the place of nouns. These replacements must be chosen carefully! Some pronouns you might use are *I, me, you, he, him, she, her, it, we, us, they, them, my, mine, your, his, her, hers, its, ours,* and *their.*

What should a little boy say when he meets a three-headed monster?

"Hello. How are <u>you</u>? Hello. How are <u>you</u>? Hello. How are <u>you</u>?"

### Show What You Know

**Read the riddles below. Circle every pronoun. You will circle six. Look at the list in *Did You Know?* if you need some help.**

Little Monster, where did (you) get that wild doll?

(I) made (it) with (my) own six little hands!

Why did the monster want to become a photographer?

(She) loved being in dark rooms.

Why did the monster cross the road?

(He) wanted to eat the chicken!

Score: _____ Total Possible: 6

116

## Practice

**Read the paragraph below. Write the correct pronoun in each blank.** Sample answers are given.

Mrs. Monster told the twins to clean

their room. ___They___ did not feel like
　　　　　　　1

cleaning. ___They___ went outside and quickly came back.
　　　　　　2

"Where did ___you___ go?" asked their mother.
　　　　　　　3

"___We___ were going to run away, but ___We/I___
　　4　　　　　　　　　　　　　　　　5

remembered that you won't let us," one monster answered.

## Revise

**Write a sentence about a funny monster.** A sample answer is given.

The monster looked scared.

**Replace the noun with a pronoun.** A sample answer is given.

He looked scared.

### Tips for Your Own Writing: Proofreading .............

Read a story you have written. Look for pronouns. Did you use pronouns in place of nouns to make the sentences sound better?

*Pronouns are exactly like substitute teachers. They are not exactly the same as the original, but they are important, too!*

117

# Lesson 57

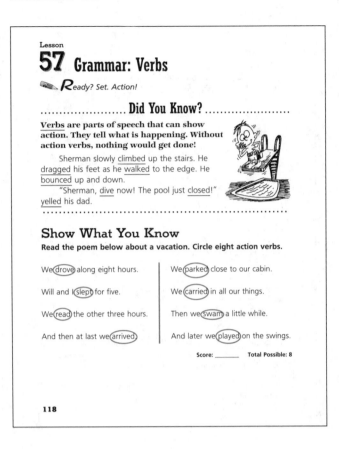

### Lesson 57 Grammar: Verbs

*Ready? Set. Action!*

#### Did You Know?

Verbs are parts of speech that can show action. They tell what is happening. Without action verbs, nothing would get done!

Sherman slowly <u>climbed</u> up the stairs. He <u>dragged</u> his feet as he <u>walked</u> to the edge. He <u>bounced</u> up and down.

"Sherman, <u>dive</u> now! The pool just <u>closed</u>!" <u>yelled</u> his dad.

#### Show What You Know

**Read the poem below about a vacation. Circle eight action verbs.**

We (drove) along eight hours.

Will and I (slept) for five.

We (read) the other three hours.

And then at last we (arrived)

We (parked) close to our cabin.

We (carried) in all our things.

Then we (swam) a little while.

And later we (played) on the swings.

Score: _____ Total Possible: 8

118

---

### Practice

**Read the paragraph below about an amusement park. Write an action verb in each blank.** Sample answers are given.

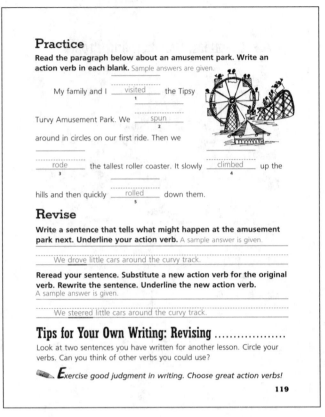

My family and I ___visited___ the Tipsy
1

Turvy Amusement Park. We ___spun___
2

around in circles on our first ride. Then we

___rode___ the tallest roller coaster. It slowly ___climbed___ up the
3                                                                4

hills and then quickly ___rolled___ down them.
5

### Revise

**Write a sentence that tells what might happen at the amusement park next. Underline your action verb.** A sample answer is given.

We drove little cars around the curvy track.

**Reread your sentence. Substitute a new action verb for the original verb. Rewrite the sentence. Underline the new action verb.**
A sample answer is given.

We steered little cars around the curvy track.

### Tips for Your Own Writing: Revising

Look at two sentences you have written for another lesson. Circle your verbs. Can you think of other verbs you could use?

*Exercise good judgment in writing. Choose great action verbs!*

119

---

# Lesson 58

### Lesson 58 Review: Nouns, Pronouns, Verbs

**A. Read the paragraph. Write a common noun in each blank.**
Sample answers are given.

Mom said that it was time to clean

my ___room___ . I had not done this for
1

two ___days___ , so I did not know what I would find. First, I looked
2

under my ___bed___ . I was surprised to see an ugly ___sock___ !
3                                                              4

After I moved the ___sock___ , I found an angry ___bug___ !
5                                                       6

Maybe I should clean my ___room___ more often.
7

Score: _____ Total Possible: 7

**B. Read the story below. Circle the proper nouns. There are seven proper nouns.**

(Tommy Twiddle) and his sister (Tess Twiddle) did not know what to do. Their favorite movie theater, (Crazy Cartoons) was closed. They went to the (Play Until Dark Park) but it was closed. Finally, (Tommy) and (Tess) rode their bikes to the (Ready to Read Library) The bike rack was full. Everyone else was looking for something to do, too!

Score: _____ Total Possible: 7

120

---

**C. Read the story below. Underline the thirteen pronouns. Look at *Did You Know?* on page 116 if you need help remembering pronouns.**

The knight was upset. <u>He</u> did not

know what to do. The king and queen

commanded <u>him</u> to find a dragon. <u>They</u> wanted to put <u>it</u> in the Royal

Zoo. The poor knight knew that no dragons existed. <u>They</u> had not lived

for many years. <u>He</u> sadly sat down on a rock.

Hours passed. An idea came to <u>him</u> when a dragonfly landed next

to <u>him</u>. He picked <u>it</u> up and brought <u>it</u> to the king and queen. <u>They</u> were

satisfied and happy. <u>They</u> had their dragon at last!

Score: _____ Total Possible: 13

**D. Read the sentences. Draw a circle around each action verb.**

1. Dr. Brainwave (made) a machine.

2. He (walked) inside.

3. What (happened) to the doctor?

4. He (felt) his head spinning!

5. His tummy (turned) flip-flops!

6. The doctor (broke) the machine.

Score: _____ Total Possible: 6

REVIEW SCORE: _____ REVIEW TOTAL: 33

121

# Lesson 59

### Lesson
# 59 Grammar: Adjectives

*Describe yourself. Wow! You are already using adjectives!*

.................... **Did You Know?** ....................

**Adjectives describe nouns and pronouns. They are parts of speech that help paint a picture in your mind.**

The young, female magician wears a tall, red, polka-dotted hat. She is standing on a big stage. The room is dark.

**An adjective can fit in the blanks in this sentence: The _____ dog is very _____.**

.............................................................

## Show What You Know

**Read the poem below. Circle eleven adjectives. If you want to test a word, use the last sentence from *Did You Know?*.**

Madge was a (good) magician.

She did (amazing) tricks.

She changed the (small) (blue) eggs

Into (little) (purple) chicks!

Madge put her (magic) wand

On a (funny) (yellow) flower.

It changed into a (green) weed.

It grew (taller) by the hour!

Score: _____    Total Possible: 11

**122**

## Practice

**Read the paragraph below. Write different adjectives in each blank.** Sample answers are given.

Maybe I can become a _famous_ (1) magician. I will need a _tall_ (2) hat and a _magic_ (3) wand. I will wear a _long_ (4) cape. After I say _funny_ (5) words, I will make a _white_ (6) rabbit appear. I will even make my _difficult_ (7) homework disappear.

## Revise

**Write one sentence about a magic trick you could perform if you were a magician. Be sure to use at least one adjective.**
A sample answer is given.

I could make a black cat disappear.

**Reread your sentence. Can you think of another adjective to add? Now rewrite the sentence with the new adjective.**
A sample answer is given.

I could make a big, black cat disappear.

## Tips for Your Own Writing: Revising ...................

Look at a story you have written. Can you make your sentences say more by adding adjectives?

*Adjectives spark your imagination! They can change words into a magical picture in your mind!*

**123**

# Lesson 60

### Lesson
# 60 Grammar: Adverbs

*On your mark. Get set. Go! Go fast! Go quickly! Go rapidly!*

.................... **Did You Know?** ....................

**Adverbs are parts of speech that describe verbs. They help you "see" the action more clearly. Adverbs often answer the questions "How?" or "Where?". Find your verb, then ask "How?" or "Where?".**

The alligator is diving into the pool.
The alligator is diving down into the pool.
Where is the alligator diving? Down!

The rooster crowed.
The rooster crowed boldly.
How did the rooster crow? Boldly.

.............................................................

## Show What You Know

**Read the sentences. Circle every adverb. There are five adverbs.**

1. The elephant pedaled (slowly) on the exercise bike.

2. The wolves (quickly) passed the football.

3. The monkey swung the bat (evenly) with its tail.

4. The crocodile fished (silently) without getting a bite.

5. The fish giggled (noisily) when the fisherman went home with nothing.

Score: _____    Total Possible: 5

**124**

## Practice

**Read the paragraph below. Write different adverbs in each blank.** Sample answers are given.

The animals were competing _nicely_ (1) in track-and-field events. The kangaroo hopped _up_ (2) over the high-jump pole. The cheetah raced _rapidly_ (3) to win the sprint. The turtle moved _slowly_ (4) in the marathon. The frog jumped _ahead_ (5) in the long jump.

## Revise

**Write one sentence about another sport an animal might do.**
A sample answer is given.

The elephant tossed the shot put.

**Reread your sentence. Look at your verb and ask "How?" and "Where?" Rewrite your sentence with the adverb.**
A sample answer is given.

The elephant easily tossed the shot put.

## Tips for Your Own Writing: Proofreading .............

Next time you write a letter about something you did, remember to use adverbs. They will help your reader picture what you did.

*Adverbs, like adjectives, trigger your imagination! Adverbs help you see vividly what is happening!*

**125**

# Lesson 61

## Lesson 61 Review: Adjectives, Adverbs

**A. Underline seventeen adjectives in the poem below.**

Biscuit was a <u>happy</u> dog.

She had a <u>lovely</u> home.

It had <u>blue</u> shingles on the roof

and <u>pink</u> pillows made of foam.

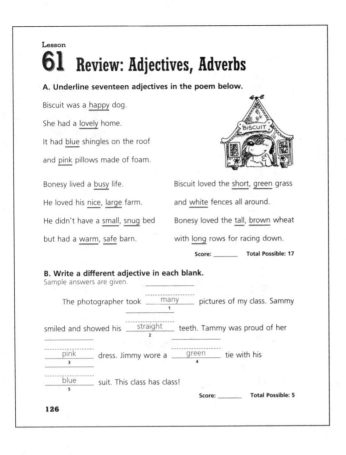

Bonesy lived a <u>busy</u> life.

He loved his <u>nice</u>, <u>large</u> farm.

He didn't have a <u>small</u>, <u>snug</u> bed

but had a <u>warm</u>, <u>safe</u> barn.

Biscuit loved the <u>short</u>, <u>green</u> grass

and <u>white</u> fences all around.

Bonesy loved the <u>tall</u>, <u>brown</u> wheat

with <u>long</u> rows for racing down.

Score: _____    Total Possible: 17

**B. Write a different adjective in each blank.**
Sample answers are given.

The photographer took <u>many</u> (1) pictures of my class. Sammy smiled and showed his <u>straight</u> (2) teeth. Tammy was proud of her <u>pink</u> (3) dress. Jimmy wore a <u>green</u> (4) tie with his <u>blue</u> (5) suit. This class has class!

Score: _____    Total Possible: 5

**126**

---

**C. Draw a circle around the adverbs. There are five adverbs.**

My baby brother Brian cried (loudly) all night. I tossed (quietly) in my bed. I (quickly) pulled the covers over my head. I heard Mother singing (softly) to Brian. I (hardly) slept.

Score: _____    Total Possible: 5

**D. Have you ever had to get up early to do something? The person in this story is having a hard time getting up. Add adverbs to make the story easier to imagine.**
Sample answers are given.

I did not hear the alarm ringing <u>quietly</u> (1). I slept <u>soundly</u> (2) in bed. Mom yelled <u>loudly</u> (3) to wake me. First, I <u>slowly</u> (4) opened my eyes. Then, I <u>silently</u> (5) climbed out of bed. I <u>quickly</u> (6) got dressed. I <u>hurriedly</u> (7) ate breakfast and <u>noisily</u> (8) brushed my teeth. I was finally ready to go fishing with my grandpa.

Score: _____    Total Possible: 8

REVIEW SCORE: _____    REVIEW TOTAL: 35

**127**

---

# Lesson 62

## Lesson 62 Grammar: Statements

*I am a statement. I do not ask. I do not yell. I just tell.*

### ...................... Did You Know? ......................

A statement is a sentence that tells something. Its first word begins with a capital letter. The sentence ends with a period.

The old robot is rusty.
The lights are not so perky.
The gears are really dusty.
The arms and legs are jerky.

The new robot is smart.
It is twice the old one's size.
It can see in darkest dark.
It has brighter, shiny eyes.

### Show What You Know

Read the paragraph below. Begin the first word of the nine statements with a capital letter. Put a period at the end of each one. Draw a circle around each period.

P
poor Robby Robot had a bad day⊙ H he swallowed a yo-yo⊙ H he thought

H
that a computer disk was a Frisbee⊙ he threw the disk out the window⊙

Robby heard a funny joke⊙ H he laughed his head off⊙ Robby went to bed⊙

H        H
he could not fall asleep⊙ he could not close his eyes⊙

**128**        Score: _____    Total Possible: 16

---

### Practice

Write two statements about a robot you would like to have. Sample answers are given.

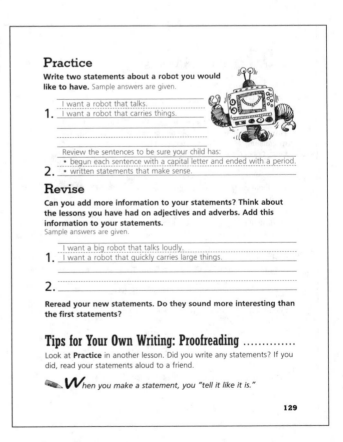

1. I want a robot that talks.
   I want a robot that carries things.

Review the sentences to be sure your child has:
• begun each sentence with a capital letter and ended with a period.
• written statements that make sense.

2.

### Revise

Can you add more information to your statements? Think about the lessons you have had on adjectives and adverbs. Add this information to your statements.
Sample answers are given.

1. I want a big robot that talks loudly.
   I want a robot that quickly carries large things.

2.

Reread your new statements. Do they sound more interesting than the first statements?

### Tips for Your Own Writing: Proofreading .............

Look at **Practice** in another lesson. Did you write any statements? If you did, read your statements aloud to a friend.

*When you make a statement, you "tell it like it is."*

**129**

---

# Lesson 63

## Lesson
# 63 Grammar: Questions

✏️ *All questions need me. What am I? I am a question mark.*

### ........................ Did You Know? ........................

A question is a sentence that asks something. Its first word begins with a capital letter. The sentence ends with a question mark.

"**W**hat will I be when I grow up?"
"Taller."

## Show What You Know

**Read the poem below. Put a question mark at the end of six sentences that ask questions.**

My class went on a boating trip.

We sailed into a stream.

Watch those beavers take a dip.

Are they a swimming team?

Our teacher said she saw a fish.

Was that a flash of gold?

Quickly we will make a wish.

Is it a magic toad?

The current took us out to sea.

What is before our eyes?

Is it a dolphin swimming free?

He sees us. Down he dives.

We must go back before too long.

Look there. Is that a shark?

Teacher says we could be wrong.

We are looking in the dark.

Score: _____ Total Possible: 6

130

## Practice

**Write two questions you would ask to learn more about something that lives in the water.**
Sample answers are given.

1. How much food does a beaver eat?
   Can a dolphin breathe underwater?

   Review the sentences to be sure your child has:
   • begun each sentence with a capital letter and ended with a question mark.
   • written questions that make sense.

2. _____

## Revise

**Rewrite one of your questions. Add more words to change the question a little.**
A sample answer is given.

What kind of food does a beaver eat?

Review the sentence to be sure your child has asked a question that makes sense.

## Tips for Your Own Writing: Proofreading .............

Look at a piece of writing you have done. Did you write any questions? Make sure you began each question with a capital letter and ended with a question mark.

✏️ *How will you ever learn the answers if you do not ask questions?*

131

---

# Lesson 64

## Lesson
# 64 Grammar: Exclamations

✏️ *Take advantage of an exclamation! Show the excitement when you write!*

### ........................ Did You Know? ........................

An exclamation is a sentence that shows surprise or excitement. Its first word begins with a capital letter. The sentence ends with an exclamation point.

**T**he octopus wants to give me a big hug!
It's like having four mothers!

## Show What You Know

**Read the poem below. Put an exclamation point at the end of three sentences that could show surprise or excitement.**
Sample answers are given.

I was in the shallow water.

A fish came swimming by.

Soon the fish had disappeared.

A shark was near. Oh, my!

He came close to show his teeth.

They were sharp and very white.

He opened up his big, big mouth.

But there was not a thing to bite!

I swam as fast as I knew how!

I was safe upon the path.

Then my mom called out to me,

"Are you finished with your bath?"

Score: _____ Total Possible: 3

132

## Practice

**Write two exciting sentences about swimming in the water. Be sure to end each with an exclamation point.**
Sample answers are given.

1. A whale swam under me!
   An octopus tried to grab me!

   Review the sentences to be sure your child has written exciting sentences that use exclamation points.

2. _____

## Revise

**Rewrite one of your exclamation sentences. Add new words to make the sentence even more exciting.** Sample answers are given.

A big whale swam under me, and its spout blasted me into the air!
An octopus tried to grab me with all eight arms!

**Read your new exclamation. Does it sound more exciting than the first time you wrote it?** Review the sentences to be sure your child has used exclamation points correctly and written sentences that make sense.

## Tips for Your Own Writing: Proofreading .............

Next time you want to share your excitement in your writing, remember to use an exclamation point.

✏️ *Exclamations are like dynamite. They can make small statements explode with excitement!*

133

# Lesson 65

### Lesson
## 65 Grammar: Commands

✎ *A command is a sentence with power. "Do something now!" it says.*

...................... **Did You Know?** ......................

A **command** is a sentence that orders. Its first word begins with a capital letter. The sentence ends with a period or an exclamation point.

Once there was a mean queen bee.
She ordered her workers around:
"**G**et me my honeycomb crown!
**F**ind flowers that are hard to see!"

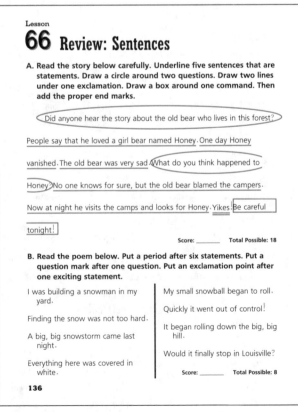

### Show What You Know

Read the conversation below. Put an exclamation point at the end of two sentences that are strong commands.
Sample answers are given.

The Queen Bee commanded, "Everyone, now get out your books. |

Open your books to page 83. Begin studying the lesson. Then, write the

words on paper."

"Why do we have to practice every day?" asked a little bee quietly.

The Queen Bee answered, "We are the proud Spelling Bees. Now

get back to work! |"

Score: _____   Total Possible: 2

134

### Practice

Write **two command sentences** that a queen or a king might say. Sample answers are given.

1. Order in the court!
   Bring me a dragon!
   Review the sentences to be sure
   your child has:
   • used commands correctly.
   • written sentences that make sense.

2. _____

### Revise

Turn one of the commands into a person's spoken command. Tell who is saying the command, and be sure to use quotation marks.

The queen said, "Bring me a dragon!"

**Read your new command aloud. How do you say the command to show the strength of the command?**

### Tips for Your Own Writing: Proofreading .............

Next time you write a story, remember to use commands. Strong commands work well if you want to show that someone is powerful.

✎ *Let a strong command be noticed! Use an exclamation point!*

135

# Lesson 66

### Lesson
## 66 Review: Sentences

**A.** Read the story below carefully. Underline five sentences that are statements. Draw a circle around two questions. Draw two lines under one exclamation. Draw a box around one command. Then add the proper end marks.

(Did anyone hear the story about the old bear who lives in this forest?)

People say that he loved a girl bear named Honey. One day Honey

vanished. The old bear was very sad. (What do you think happened to

Honey?) No one knows for sure, but the old bear blamed the campers.

Now at night he visits the camps and looks for Honey. Yikes! [Be careful

tonight!]

Score: _____   Total Possible: 18

**B.** Read the poem below. Put a period after six statements. Put a question mark after one question. Put an exclamation point after one exciting statement.

I was building a snowman in my yard.

Finding the snow was not too hard.

A big, big snowstorm came last night.

Everything here was covered in white.

My small snowball began to roll.

Quickly it went out of control!

It began rolling down the big, big hill.

Would it finally stop in Louisville?

Score: _____   Total Possible: 8

136

**C.** Read each sentence below. Decide whether it is a question, an exclamation, a command, or a statement. Circle the correct answer.

1. Take your sister to the park!

   Statement        Question        Exclamation        (Command)

2. I think a monster lives under my bed and messes up my room.

   (Statement)      Question        Exclamation        Command

3. A green space creature ate my homework!

   Statement        Question        (Exclamation)      Command

4. Did you see the dolphin leap out of the water?

   Statement        (Question)      Exclamation        Command

5. I never wear a raincoat when it rains.

   (Statement)      Question        Exclamation        Command

6. Follow me!

   Statement        Question        Exclamation        (Command)

7. Do ostriches really bury their heads in the sand?

   Statement        (Question)      Exclamation        Command

8. That gorilla stole my banana!

   Statement        Question        (Exclamation)      Command

Score: _____   Total Possible: 8

REVIEW SCORE: _____   REVIEW TOTAL: 34

137

# Lesson 67

### Lesson
## 67 Grammar: Combining Sentences— Nouns

✎ *Sometimes my friend and I use the "buddy system" when writing sentences. It can be twice as nice to do something together. Some sentences are better if they are put together.*

.................. **Did You Know?** ..................

**Some sentences tell about more than one subject. The word *and* joins the two subjects.**

Seals eat fish. <u>People</u> eat fish.
<u>Seals</u> **and** <u>people</u> eat fish.
<u>Penguins</u> wear dark suits. <u>Business people</u> wear dark suits.
<u>Penguins</u> **and** <u>business people</u> wear dark suits.

### Show What You Know

**Read each sentence below. Circle all of the subjects and the *and* that joins them.**

1. Leopards and sick children may see spots before their eyes.

2. Kangaroos and rich ladies have fur coats with big pockets.

3. Elephants and airport visitors have big trunks.

4. Rabbits and children can do the Bunny Hop.

5. Snakes and dieters bring their scales everywhere.

Score: _____   Total Possible: 5

138

### Practice

**Read each set of sentences below. Combine each set into one sentence. Look at *Did You Know?* to see how.**
Sample answers are given.

1. Bears give big hugs. Dads give big hugs.

   Bears and dads give big hugs.

2. Frogs try to catch flies. Baseball players try to catch flies.

   Frogs and baseball players try to catch flies.

3. Parrots love to talk. Teenagers love to talk.

   Parrots and teenagers love to talk.

### Revise

**Look at your sentences. Think of another animal that shares some of the traits described. Choose one sentence. Rewrite the sentence changing the original animal.** A sample answer is given.

Spiders and baseball players try to catch flies.
You may wish to brainstorm animals to give your child more to work with. Review the sentence to be sure he or she has used the conjunction correctly.

### Tips for Your Own Writing: Revising ...............

Look at a story you have written. Can you find places where two sentences talk about two people doing the same thing? Combine such sentences into one. Remember to use *and*.

✎ *Sometimes more than one person or thing does the same thing in a sentence.*

139

............................................................

# Lesson 68

### Lesson
## 68 Grammar: Combining Sentences— Verbs

✎ *Pat your nose with one hand. Rub your tummy with the other. Pat your nose and rub your tummy at the same time! Sometimes we like to do more than one thing.*

.................. **Did You Know?** ..................

**A subject can do more than one thing in a sentence. When this is true, the sentence has more than one verb. The word *and* joins these verbs.**

Little Benny <u>jumps</u> in mud puddles. Little Benny <u>gets</u> me wet.
Little Benny <u>jumps</u> in mud puddles **and** <u>gets</u> me wet.

**Sometimes you leave out words when you combine sentences.**

### Show What You Know

**Read each sentence below. Circle the two verbs and the *and* in each sentence.**

1. Barney climbs trees and eats bananas.

2. Jenny jumps on her bed and flies in the air.

3. Roland is brave and rides the fast roller coaster.

4. Sandy plays in the sand and makes sandwiches.

Score: _____   Total Possible: 12

140

### Practice

**Read each set of sentences. Combine them into one sentence. Circle the two verbs and the *and* that join each set.**
Sample answers are given.

1. Samantha eats snacks all night. Samantha watches TV all night.

   Samantha eats snacks and watches TV all night.

2. Todd jumps for the ball. Todd catches the ball.

   Todd jumps for the ball and catches the ball.

3. Marsha goes to the movies. Marsha eats popcorn.

   Marsha goes to the movies and eats popcorn.

### Revise

**Choose one of the sentences. Change one of the verbs. Write the new sentence.**

Marsha goes to the movies and buys popcorn.
Review the sentence to be sure your child has used the conjunction correctly and deleted unnecessary words.

### Tips for Your Own Writing: Revising ...............

Look at a sentence you wrote for a **Practice** in another lesson. Find the subject and think how it could do more than one thing. Write the new sentence. Ask an adult to look at your work.

✎ *Sometimes a person rereads sentences and leaves out some words to turn two sentences into one.*

141

# Lesson 69

### Lesson
# 69 Grammar: Combining Sentences– Adjectives

*Words that describe paint a picture. They help you see the sentence more clearly in your mind.*

........................ **Did You Know?** ........................

By taking a describing word from one sentence and adding it to another, you help paint a better picture of the sentence.

> I wore my tennis shoes to the picnic.
> My shoes are **new.**
> I wore my **new** tennis shoes to the picnic.

A word that describes a noun is called an <u>adjective.</u>

..............................................................

## Show What You Know

**Read each sentence. Circle the describing word in the second sentence. Draw an arrow to show where it fits in the first sentence.**

**Example:** We ate a watermelon and spit out the seeds.

> The watermelon was (juicy.)

1. The boys and girls raced in sacks.

> The sacks were (burlap.)

2. We flew kites high in the air.

> The kites were (plastic.)

Score: _____ Total Possible: 4

142

## Practice

**Read each set of sentences. Circle the describing word. Write a new sentence by adding the describing word from the second sentence into the first.**

**Example:** I read a fairy tale. The fairy tale was (short.)
> I read a **short** fairy tale.

1. Rapunzel lived in a tower. The tower was (tall.)

> Rapunzel lived in a tall tower.

2. A witch moved Rapunzel to the forest. A witch was (mean.)

> A mean witch moved Rapunzel to the forest.

3. The prince walked <u>through</u> a forest and found Rapunzel. The forest was (dangerous.)

> The prince walked through a dangerous forest and found Rapunzel.

## Revise

**Choose one of the new sentences. Add one more describing word.**
A sample answer is given.
> The mean, ugly witch moved Rapunzel to the forest.

## Tips for Your Own Writing: Revising ...................

Look at a story you have written. Can you find adjectives you used? Can you find a way to combine these adjectives with other sentences?

*You can write a sentence. The sentence is important. Can you combine your ideas? Then you can write an important sentence.*

143

---

# Lesson 70

### Lesson
# 70 Combining Sentences–Adverbs

*How do you eat—slowly, quickly, quietly, or loudly? This really can make a difference to the person sitting next to you!*

...................... **Did You Know?** ......................

Words that describe actions or verbs are called <u>adverbs.</u> Adverbs help you see action more <u>clearly</u> in your mind. Sometimes you can take a word describing an action from one sentence and add it to another.

> The elephant stood on her back feet.
> She stood **tall.**
> The elephant stood **tall** on her back feet.

..............................................................

## Show What You Know

**Read each sentence below. Circle the describing word in the second sentence. Draw an arrow to show where it fits best in the first sentence.**

**Example:** A monkey flipped in the air off the back of a horse.

> It flipped (high.)

1. A pretty lady spun on a rope.

> She spun (around.)

2. A little clown stepped on the giant clown's toes.

> He stepped (hard.)

Score: _____ Total Possible: 4

144

## Practice

**Read each set of sentences below. Underline the describing word in the second sentence. Then, write a new sentence by adding the describing word from the second sentence into the first.**

**Example:** We planned a circus in our yard. We <u>carefully</u> planned it. We carefully planned a circus in our yard.

1. My puppy Gizmo growled like a lion. He growled <u>loudly.</u>

> My puppy, Gizmo, growled loudly like a lion.

2. Jill's cat Tiger jumped through the hoops. Tiger jumped <u>quickly.</u>

> Jill's cat, Tiger, jumped quickly through the hoops.

3. Brad's snake Pretzel twisted into many shapes. It twisted <u>slowly.</u>

> Brad's snake, Pretzel, twisted slowly into many shapes.

## Revise

**Choose one of your sentences. Add one more describing word to the action.** A sample answer is given.
> My puppy, Gizmo, growled bravely and loudly like a lion.

## Tips for Your Own Writing: Proofreading .............

Look at your writing. Did you remember to add describing words to the action part of your sentence and use correct capitalization and punctuation?

*Make the words describing your actions "jump off" the paper.*

145

### Lesson 71 — Grammar: Combining Sentences—Objects

*Go for the gold and the silver! Be like an Olympic athlete. It's fun to choose a variety of goals!*

...................... Did You Know? ......................

A sentence can give information about something or someone. This information comes after the verb. When there is more than one piece of information, it is joined by the word *and*.

This stork delivers babies.
This stork delivers Cabbage Patch Dolls.
This stork delivers <u>babies</u> **and** <u>Cabbage Patch Dolls</u>.

### Show What You Know

**Read each sentence below. Underline the verb first. Then circle the words that give more information about the verb.**

1. Tooth fairies <u>carry</u> (coins) and many (teeth)
2. Horseshoes <u>give</u> (luck) and (foot support)
3. Genies <u>grant</u> (wishes) and (desires)
4. A flying carpet <u>transports</u> (magic dust) and (people)
5. A leprechaun <u>wants</u> (gold) and (power)

Score: _____ Total Possible: 15

146

### Practice

**Read each set of sentences below. Combine the objects in both sentences into one smooth sentence.** Sample answers are given.

1. Elves make shoes. Elves make toys.
   Elves make shoes and toys.

2. Magicians have magic wands. Magicians have magic hats.
   Magicians have magic wands and magic hats.

3. Rabbits make colored eggs. Rabbits make chocolate bunnies.
   Rabbits make colored eggs and chocolate bunnies.

4. Mermaids like oysters' pearls. Mermaids like sea creatures.
   Mermaids like oysters' pearls and sea creatures.

### Revise

**Choose one of your sentences. Replace one of the objects.**
A sample answer is given.
   Magicians have magic wands and rabbits.
   Review the sentences to be sure your child has used objects correctly.

### Tips for Your Own Writing: Proofreading ..............

Next time you write a letter, try to give a lot of information about your verbs. You can do this by adding nouns after the verb.

*Sometimes we need patience and hard work to make an interesting sentence.*

147

...................................................................

### Lesson 72 — Review: Combining Sentences

**A. Combine the nouns in each set of sentences into one sentence.**
Sample answers are given.
1. Pianos have lots of keys. Custodians have lots of keys.
   Pianos and custodians have lots of keys.

2. Mail carriers have many letters. Alphabets have many letters.
   Mail carriers and alphabets have many letters.

3. Sometimes children lose their teeth. Sometimes combs lose their teeth.
   Sometimes children and combs lose their teeth.

Score: _____ Total Possible: 3

**B. Combine each set of sentences into one sentence. Concentrate on the verbs.** Sample answers are given.

1. Big Foot wears super-sized sneakers. Big Foot takes great big steps.
   Big Foot wears super-sized sneakers and takes great big steps.

2. Little Bo Peep lost her sheep. Little Bo Peep bought a new leash.
   Little Bo Peep lost her sheep and bought a new leash.

3. The little old woman lived in a shoe. The little old woman got the heel fixed.
   The little old woman lived in a shoe and got the heel fixed.

Score: _____ Total Possible: 3

148

**C. Put the describing word (adjective) from the second sentence into the first. Write the new sentence.**
1. Buster rode his bike on the path. His bike is muddy.
   Buster rode his muddy bike on the path.

2. Goldie Goodheart loves her puppy. The puppy is playful.
   Goldie Goodheart loves her playful puppy.

Score: _____ Total Possible: 2

**D. Add the describing word or adverb from the second sentence into the first sentence. Write the new sentence.**
1. The centipede put shoes on her feet. She carefully put them on.
   The centipede carefully put shoes on her feet.

2. The fuzzy caterpillar changed into a butterfly. It slowly changed.
   The fuzzy caterpillar changed slowly into a butterfly.

Score: _____ Total Possible: 2

**E. Look for the words after the verbs. Find a way to combine the sentences into a single sentence.** Sample answers are given.
1. Big Moose eats banana splits. Big Moose eats hamburgers.
   Big Moose eats banana splits and hamburgers.

2. Charlie Chuckles tells lots of jokes. Charlie Chuckles tells many riddles.
   Charlie Chuckles tells lots of jokes and many riddles.

Score: _____ Total Possible: 2
REVIEW SCORE: _____ REVIEW TOTAL: 12

149

# Proofreading Marks

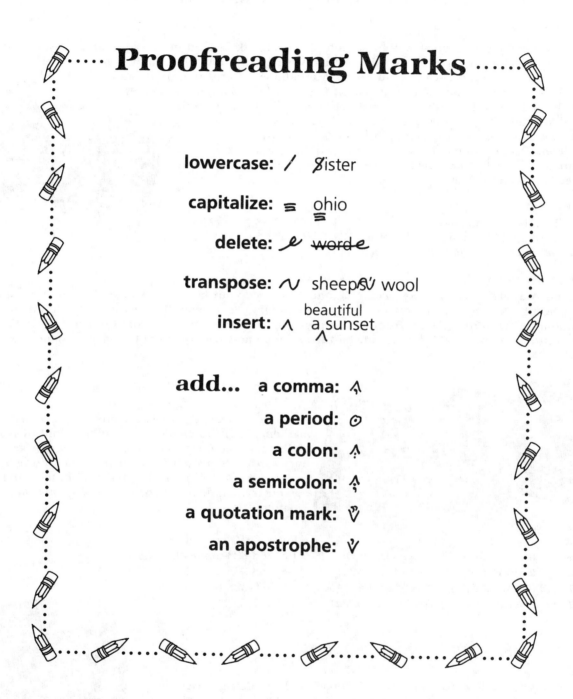

lowercase: / $\cancel{S}$ister

capitalize: ☰ o̲h̲i̲o̲

delete: ℓ ~~word~~e

transpose: ∾ sheep∾ wool

insert: ∧ $\overset{\text{beautiful}}{\text{a} \wedge \text{sunset}}$

add...   a comma: ⩟

a period: ⊙

a colon: ⩚

a semicolon: ⩘

a quotation mark: ⱴ

an apostrophe: ⱴ

## McGraw-Hill Consumer Products

The skills taught in school are now available at home!
These award-winning software titles meet school guidelines and are based on
The McGraw-Hill Companies classroom software titles.

### MATH GRADES 1 & 2

These math programs are a great way to teach and reinforce skills used in everyday situations. Fun, friendly characters need help with their math skills. Everyone's friend, Nubby the stubby pencil, will help kids master the math in the Numbers Quiz show. Foggy McHammer, a carpenter, needs some help building his playhouse so that all the boards will fit together! Julio Bambino's kitchen antics will surely burn his pastries if you don't help him set the clock timer correctly! We can't forget Turbo Tomato, a fruit with a passion for adventure, who needs help calculating his daredevil stunts.

Math Grades 1 & 2 use a tested, proven approach to reinforcing your child's math skills while keeping him or her intrigued with Nubby and his collection of crazy friends.

| TITLE | ISBN | PRICE |
|---|---|---|
| Grade 1: Nubby's Quiz Show | 1-57768-321-8 | $9.95 |
| Grade 2: Foggy McHammer's Treehouse | 1-57768-322-6 | $9.95 |

*Available in jewel case only (no box included)*

### MISSION MASTERS™ MATH AND LANGUAGE ARTS

The Mission Masters™—Pauline, Rakeem, Mia, and T.J.—need your help. The Mission Masters™ are a team of young agents working for the Intelliforce Agency, a high-level cooperative whose goal is to maintain order on our rather unruly planet. From within the agency's top secret Command Control Center, the agency's central computer, M5, has detected a threat...and guess what—you're the agent assigned to the mission!

### MISSION MASTERS™ MATH GRADES 3, 4, & 5

This series of exciting activities encourages young mathematicians to challenge themselves and their math skills to overcome the perils of villains and other planetary threats. Skills reinforced include: analyzing and solving real-world problems, estimation, measurements, geometry, whole numbers, fractions, graphs, and patterns.

| TITLE | ISBN | PRICE |
|---|---|---|
| Grade 3: Mission Masters™ Defeat Dirty D! | 1-57768-323-5 | $9.95 |
| Grade 4: Mission Masters™ Alien Encounter | 1-57768-324-2 | $9.95 |
| Grade 5: Mission Masters™ Meet Mudflat Moe | 1-57768-325-0 | $9.95 |

*Available in jewel case only (no box included)*

### MISSION MASTERS™ LANGUAGE ARTS GRADES 3, 4, & 5

This series invites children to apply their language skills to defeat unscrupulous characters and to overcome other earthly dangers. Skills reinforced include: language mechanics and usage, punctuation, spelling, vocabulary, reading comprehension, and creative writing.

| TITLE | ISBN | PRICE |
|---|---|---|
| Grade 3: Mission Masters™ Freezing Frenzy | 1-57768-343-9 | $9.95 |
| Grade 4: Mission Masters™ Network Nightmare | 1-57768-344-7 | $9.95 |
| Grade 5: Mission Masters™ Mummy Mysteries | 1-57768-345-5 | $9.95 |

*Available in jewel case only (no box included)*

## BASIC SKILLS BUILDER K to 2 – THE MAGIC APPLEHOUSE

At the Magic Applehouse, children discover that Abigail Appleseed runs a deliciously successful business selling apple pies, tarts, and other apple treats. Enthusiasm grows as children join in the fun of helping Abigail run her business. Along the way they'll develop computer and entrepreneurial skills to last a lifetime. They will run their own business – all while they're having bushels of fun!

| TITLE | ISBN | PRICE |
|-------|------|-------|
| Basic Skills Builder –The Magic Applehouse | 1-57768-312-9 | $9.95 |

*Available in jewel case only (no box included)*

## TEST PREP – SCORING HIGH

This grade-based testing software will help prepare your child for standardized achievement tests given by his or her school. Scoring High specifically targets the skills required for success on the Stanford Achievement Test (SAT) for grades three through eight. Lessons and test questions follow the same format and cover the same content areas as questions appearing on the actual SAT tests. The practice tests are modeled after the SAT test-taking experience with similar directions, number of questions per section, and bubble-sheet answer choices.

Scoring High is a child's first-class ticket to a winning score on standardized achievement tests!

| TITLE | ISBN | PRICE |
|-------|------|-------|
| Grades 3 to 5: Scoring High Test Prep | 1-57768-316-1 | $9.95 |
| Grades 6 to 8: Scoring High Test Prep | 1-57768-317-X | $9.95 |

*Available in jewel case only (no box included)*

## SCIENCE

Mastering the principles of both physical and life science has never been so FUN for kids grades six and above as it is while they are exploring McGraw-Hill's edutainment software!

| TITLE | ISBN | PRICE |
|-------|------|-------|
| Grades 6 & up: Life Science | 1-57768-336-6 | $9.95 |
| Grades 8 & up: Physical Science | 1-57768-308-0 | $9.95 |

*Available in jewel case only (no box included)*

## REFERENCE

The National Museum of Women in the Arts has teamed with McGraw-Hill Consumer Products to bring you this superb collection available for your enjoyment on CD-ROM.

This special collection is a visual diary of 200 women artists from the Renaissance to the present, spanning 500 years of creativity.

You will discover the art of women who excelled in all the great art movements of history. Artists who pushed the boundaries of abstract, genre, landscape, narrative, portrait, and still-life styles; as well as artists forced to push the societal limits placed on women through the ages.

| TITLE | ISBN | PRICE |
|-------|------|-------|
| Women in the Arts | 1-57768-010-3 | $29.95 |

*Available in boxed version only*

*Most titles for Windows 3.1™, Windows '95™ & '98™, and Macintosh™.*

**Visit us on the Internet at:**

# www.MHkids.com

Or call 800-298-4119 for your local retailer.

All our workbooks meet school curriculum guidelines and correspond to The McGraw-Hill Companies classroom textbooks.

# SPECTRUM SERIES

## DOLCH Sight Word Activities

The DOLCH Sight Word Activities Workbooks use the classic Dolch list of 220 basic vocabulary words that make up from 50% to 75% of all reading matter that children ordinarily encounter. Since these words are ordinarily recognized on sight, they are called *sight words*. Volume 1 includes 110 sight words. Volume 2 covers the remainder of the list. Over 160 pages.

| TITLE | ISBN | PRICE |
|---|---|---|
| Grades K-1 Vol. 1 | 1-57768-429-X | $9.95 |
| Grades K-1 Vol. 2 | 1-57768-439-7 | $9.95 |

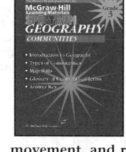

## GEOGRAPHY

Full-color, three-part lessons strengthen geography knowledge and map reading skills. Focusing on five geographic themes including location, place, human/environmental interaction, movement, and regions. Over 150 pages. Glossary of geographical terms and answer key included.

| TITLE | ISBN | PRICE |
|---|---|---|
| Gr 3, Communities | 1-57768-153-3 | $7.95 |
| Gr 4, Regions | 1-57768-154-1 | $7.95 |
| Gr 5, USA | 1-57768-155-X | $7.95 |
| Gr 6, World | 1-57768-156-8 | $7.95 |

## MATH

Features easy-to-follow instructions that give students a clear path to success. This series has comprehensive coverage of the basic skills, helping children to master math fundamentals. Over 150 pages. Answer key included.

| TITLE | ISBN | PRICE |
|---|---|---|
| Grade 1 | 1-57768-111-8 | $7.95 |
| Grade 2 | 1-57768-112-6 | $7.95 |
| Grade 3 | 1-57768-113-4 | $7.95 |
| Grade 4 | 1-57768-114-2 | $7.95 |
| Grade 5 | 1-57768-115-0 | $7.95 |
| Grade 6 | 1-57768-116-9 | $7.95 |
| Grade 7 | 1-57768-117-7 | $7.95 |
| Grade 8 | 1-57768-118-5 | $7.95 |

## PHONICS

Provides everything children need to build multiple skills in language. Focusing on phonics, structural analysis, and dictionary skills, this series also offers creative ideas for using phonics and word study skills in other language arts. Over 200 pages. Answer key included.

| TITLE | ISBN | PRICE |
|---|---|---|
| Grade K | 1-57768-120-7 | $7.95 |
| Grade 1 | 1-57768-121-5 | $7.95 |
| Grade 2 | 1-57768-122-3 | $7.95 |
| Grade 3 | 1-57768-123-1 | $7.95 |
| Grade 4 | 1-57768-124-X | $7.95 |
| Grade 5 | 1-57768-125-8 | $7.95 |
| Grade 6 | 1-57768-126-6 | $7.95 |

## READING

This full-color series creates an enjoyable reading environment, even for below-average readers. Each book contains captivating content, colorful characters, and compelling illustrations, so children are eager to find out what happens next. Over 150 pages. Answer key included.

| TITLE | ISBN | PRICE |
|---|---|---|
| Grade K | 1-57768-130-4 | $7.95 |
| Grade 1 | 1-57768-131-2 | $7.95 |
| Grade 2 | 1-57768-132-0 | $7.95 |
| Grade 3 | 1-57768-133-9 | $7.95 |
| Grade 4 | 1-57768-134-7 | $7.95 |
| Grade 5 | 1-57768-135-5 | $7.95 |
| Grade 6 | 1-57768-136-3 | $7.95 |

## SPELLING

This full-color series links spelling to reading and writing and increases skills in words and meanings, consonant and vowel spellings, and proofreading practice. Over 200 pages. Speller dictionary and answer key included.

| TITLE | ISBN | PRICE |
|---|---|---|
| Grade 1 | 1-57768-161-4 | $7.95 |
| Grade 2 | 1-57768-162-2 | $7.95 |
| Grade 3 | 1-57768-163-0 | $7.95 |
| Grade 4 | 1-57768-164-9 | $7.95 |
| Grade 5 | 1-57768-165-7 | $7.95 |
| Grade 6 | 1-57768-166-5 | $7.95 |

## WRITING

Lessons focus on creative and expository writing using clearly stated objectives and pre-writing exercises. Eight essential reading skills are applied. Activities include main idea, sequence, comparison, detail, fact and opinion, cause and effect, and making a point. Over 130 pages. Answer key included.

| TITLE | ISBN | PRICE |
|---|---|---|
| Grade 1 | 1-57768-141-X | $7.95 |
| Grade 2 | 1-57768-142-8 | $7.95 |
| Grade 3 | 1-57768-143-6 | $7.95 |
| Grade 4 | 1-57768-144-4 | $7.95 |
| Grade 5 | 1-57768-145-2 | $7.95 |
| Grade 6 | 1-57768-146-0 | $7.95 |
| Grade 7 | 1-57768-147-9 | $7.95 |
| Grade 8 | 1-57768-148-7 | $7.95 |

## TEST PREP
### From the Nation's #1 Testing Company

Prepares children to do their best on current editions of the five major standardized tests. Activities reinforce test-taking skills through examples, tips, practice, and timed exercises. Subjects include reading, math, and language. Over 150 pages. Answer key included.

| TITLE | ISBN | PRICE |
|---|---|---|
| Grade 1 | 1-57768-101-0 | $8.95 |
| Grade 2 | 1-57768-102-9 | $8.95 |
| Grade 3 | 1-57768-103-7 | $8.95 |
| Grade 4 | 1-57768-104-5 | $8.95 |
| Grade 5 | 1-57768-105-3 | $8.95 |
| Grade 6 | 1-57768-106-1 | $8.95 |
| Grade 7 | 1-57768-107-X | $8.95 |
| Grade 8 | 1-57768-108-8 | $8.95 |

## LANGUAGE ARTS

Encourages creativity and builds confidence by making writing fun! Seventy-two four-part lessons strengthen writing skills by focusing on parts of speech, word usage, sentence structure, punctuation, and proofreading. Each level includes a *Writer's Handbook* at the end of the book that offers writing tips. This series is based on the highly respected SRA/McGraw-Hill language arts series. More than 180 full-color pages. *Available March 2000.*

| TITLE | ISBN | PRICE |
|---|---|---|
| Grade 2 | 1-57768-472-9 | $7.95 |
| Grade 3 | 1-57768-473-7 | $7.95 |
| Grade 4 | 1-57768-474-5 | $7.95 |
| Grade 5 | 1-57768-475-3 | $7.95 |
| Grade 6 | 1-57768-476-1 | $7.95 |

# CERTIFICATE OF ACCOMPLISHMENT

*THIS CERTIFIES THAT*

*HAS SUCCESSFULLY COMPLETED*

# SPECTRUM
## *Language Arts*
## *Grade 2*
### *WORKBOOK*

*CONGRATULATIONS AND KEEP UP THE GOOD WORK!*

*McGraw-Hill*
**Consumer Products**
A Division of The McGraw-Hill Companies

*Publisher*